INSIGHT PO

COSTA BLANCA

APA PUBLICATIONS

Part of the Langenscheidt Publishing Group

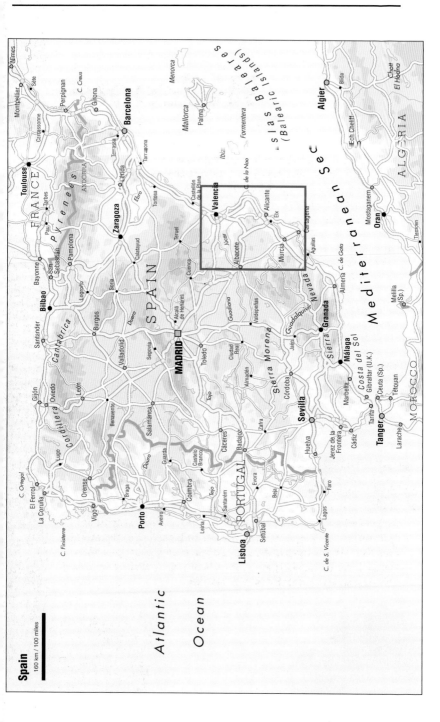

Welcome

This guidebook combines the interests and enthusiasms of two of the world's best-known information providers: Insight Guides, who have set the standard for visual travel guides since 1970, and Discovery Channel, the world's premier source of nonfiction television programming. Its aim is to bring you the best of the Costa Blanca, famous for its blue skies, white beaches and warm Mediterranean waters. The book covers not only today's Costa Blanca – the Alicante coastline – but also the southern stretch that was once part of it, and now has its own identity and popularity as the Costa Cálida.

In a series of tailor-made itineraries devised by Insight's correspondent, Vicky Hayward, we take you behind the busy resorts and cities of the coast to explore the "real" Spain in the hinterland of the Alicante and Murcia regions: fertile valleys, historic towns, spectacular sierras and fine baroque architecture. The itineraries are divided into three sections; The North, covering the northern areas of Alicante region and southern Valencia; The Centre, which details the rest of Alicante region; and The South, which covers the Murcia region. There is also a section on leisure activities, including shopping, eating and drinking, nightlife, beaches and sport; and a practical basics section with a list of recommended hotels. With the use of Valenciano as well as Castilian Spanish in the region, there are variant spellings for some towns – a full explanation of spellings used in this guide can be found on page 96.

Vicky Hayward lives in Madrid, working as a freelance writer and journalist. She first got to know this coast as a child on family holidays: 'One of my clearest childhood memories of Spain is of a drive south to Alicante in the early 1960s. My brother and I spent the journey leaning out of the car's windows, waving at the farmers riding to the fields on their donkeys. In the first hour, our combined donkey tally reached over 200.' This journey was the start of a lasting love for a region which, though depleted of donkeys these days, still retains many unique charms. This guide shows you exactly where to find them.

HISTORY AND CULTURE

From the Iberians to the Muslims, from the Reconquest to the Spanish Civil War – key episodes in the history of this southeastern corner of Spain **11–17**

THE NORTH

THE CENTRE: ALICANTE REGION

14 Southern Costa Blanca: Alicante to Dehesa follows the coast road south from Alicante, with a boat trip to Tabarca Island **50**

THE SOUTH: MURCIA REGION

15 Murcia City: Spanish Baroque spends a day exploring Murcia's unique style of baroque art and architecture **55**

16 The Murcian Wine Country: Jumilla, Yecla and Bullas samples fine wines and churches **57**

17 Down the Segura Valley: Calasparra to Murcia City follows the Segura river from Calasparra to Murcia and down to the coast **58**

18 A Morning at a Spa dips into the therapeutic waters of a trio of traditional spa towns **61**

19 Orihuela and Lorca investigates two towns known for their architectural splendour **62**

20 The Sierras de Espuña and Moratalla explores Murcia's splendid *parque natural* and nearby villages .**65**

21 Cartagena City combines a look at Cartagena's museums and old town with a drive east to the beach at Calblanque **67**

22 La Union, Calblanque and Cabo de Palos tours the beautiful mining country and virgin beaches east of Cartagena **69**

LEISURE ACTIVITIES
What to buy, where to eat, and where to go..........**71–85**

PRACTICAL INFORMATION
All the background information you are likely to need for your stay, from getting around to money matters, including a list of hand-picked hotels **87–98**

MAPS

Spain ....**4**   *The Centre:*
Northern Costa   *Alicante Region* ..**46/47**
Blanca ....**18/19**   *The South:*
Benidorm ....**33**   *Murcia Region* **52/53**
Alicante City ....**37**   *Murcia City* **56**

INDEX AND CREDITS
pages **101–104**

Pages 2/3: the hilltop village of Polop de la Marina
Pages 8/9: Dénia's shellfish served in local style

History & Culture

A s you stroll through the crowded modern resorts of the Costa Blanca it is hard to imagine life here before tourism arrived, but the last 50 years of the area's development represents a tiny chunk of time in the span of its human history. Over 50,000 years ago the welcoming climate and landscape encouraged some of the earliest human settlements in Spain, exceptional evidence of which has survived today, despite the rash of building on the coast. There are early caves dating back to 50,000BC; more recent sites (*circa* 6,000BC) with paintings of hunting and animals, as at La Sarga, near Alcoi, and Monte Arabí, at Yecla; and magnificent Iberian treasures at Alcudia, near Elche, and Villena.

The Iberians' origins are obscure, but we know they were spread through present-day Valencia, Albacete and Murcia, living as autonomous tribes. Two cultures developed alongside one another: the Argaric to the south and Valencian to the north, with their boundary along the Vinalopo valley. Both used precious metals to make ornaments and jewellery: examples can be seen in the splendid treasures at Villena and Cigarralejo.

Iberians, Phoenicians and Romans

The Argaric and Valencian cultures merged to become the Contestani, a farming people who kept large herds of cattle, grew wheat and traded with sea-faring Phoenicians from the 8th century BC. They mined in the sierras and introduced fish-salting, the potter's wheel, the date palm, vine, fig and olive. Then, in the 5th century BC, the Massiliot Greeks charted the coast and built settlements along it. Adapting these Mediterranean influences, the Iberians produced decorated ceramics and sculptures, including the *Dama de Elche*, one of a series of stone carvings linked to the worship of a mother/fertility goddess.

After the western Phoenician colonies lost the first Punic War, they extended their power in southern Spain, triggering Iberian resistance and, in 218BC, Roman invasion. The army moved slowly south from present-day Catalunya, nine years later conquering the Carthaginian capital Quart Hades, which the Romans renamed Cartago Nova – today Cartagena.

Here in Hispania Citerior Roman generals wintered, fish-salting factories were built, a road network and irrigation systems were developed and wine, olive oil and wheat were produced for export to Rome. The lead and silver mines behind Cartago Nova employed 40,000 Iberian slaves. Great tracts of forest, chopped down to provide timber, were replaced by *esparto* grass (used to make bags) and the city was renamed Cartago Espartaria.

Left: 16th-century map of the region
Right: the *Dama de Elche* stone carving

In the decline before the collapse of Roman power in the 5th century, many towns were either abandoned and replaced by rural settlements, or changed site, moving – like Lucentum (Alicante) – to more defensive positions. By the middle of the 7th century Lucentum had fallen, like the rest of the country, to the Visigoths.

The Arab Conquest

Just as the Romans had invited the Visigoths to help them keep order, so a dynastic Visigothic squabble opened the door to a Muslim takeover of the peninsula in 711–14. Tribes and dynasties from various parts of the Arab world invaded and ruled in succession. Meanwhile the power structure shifted from a potent caliphate, set up in Córdoba in the 8th century, to the *taifas*, or splinter kingdoms of the 11th century, and then to military control by the Almoravids and Almohads – Berber tribes from the Atlas mountains who invaded in the 12th century.

The landscape was transformed by Muslim irrigation techniques. Their water wheels and irrigation channels in the river valleys allowed the widespread cultivation of oranges, lemons, almonds and rice, which still forms the basis of the region's agricultural economy. Under the *taifas*, the flowering of urban culture and craft workshops – paper manufacture and silk-making, boat-building and ceramics – was to provide the basis of the medieval urban economy and, much later, the region's first industries.

Rural hamlets (*quaryas*), called *alquerías* by the Spanish, were protected and controlled by a network of castles, and planned in a pattern that has remained to this day in the Ricote and Gallinera valleys. Murcia city, founded in the 9th century, acquired power as the head of a *taifa* stretching north to Alicante, and briefly became the capital of al-Andalus in the 13th century; Dénia, the second city of the region and capital of another *taifa*, grew to a population of around 50,000 and was a cultural centre. Orihuela and Alcoy – both with a large number of cloth and dye workshops – Xàtiva, Cocentaina and Lorca became important as commercial and administrative centres.

When the Christian Reconquest finally started in the 13th century, it moved swiftly southwards in a two-pronged drive by Castile and Aragon, more often taking the form of local surrender pacts than military victories. The treaties carving up the new territories moved the Aragonese border south. The 1304 Treaty of Torrellas fixed the border for the next 500 years, dividing the old kingdom of Murcia in half, with Orihuela and the lower Segura valley passing to Aragon and the rump remaining for Castile.

As social history, the Reconquest was a much slower process, with resettlement continuing in uneven spurts until the 18th century. Most large towns had begun to take on less defensive profiles by the end of the 14th century. Separate Muslim and Christian quarters typically

Left: many castles combine Arab and Christian military architecture

spilled down from the protection of the castle rearing above them; Cocentaina is the clearest surviving example of this layout, with the Raval and Villa still quite distinct. Churches, often on the sites of 'purified' mosques, usually took more than several centuries to build due to lack of funds. The cathedral at Orihuela is one of the best examples of spacious late Gothic elements overlaid by trimmings in florid late Isabelline Gothic and 16th-century Plateresque. In the countryside, vineyards were planted to meet the new demand for wine.

The palaces and castles reflected the growing division of the reconquered territories into señorial power blocs. The Marquesado de Villena, a state-within-a-state owing allegiance to Castile, was the most powerful of these, but huge tracts of land were granted to other noble families too over the course of time: Onil, Ibi, Castalla and Albatera went to the Marqueses de las Dos Aguas from Valencia; Cocentaina, Callosa and Benidorm to the de Laurias from Catalunya; great chunks of Murcia to the Marqueses of Vélez. Likewise, the southern frontier towns around the Sierra de Espuña were for centuries ruled by the Orders of the Knights Templar and Santiago. The privileges of such absentee landlords came to be bitterly resented.

Castile and Aragon United

It was only after the union of Castile and Aragon through the marriage of Isabella and Ferdinand (1474) that the nobility began to cooperate with the Church and state. Aragon's trades – cloth, metalwork, leather, furniture making and boat building – grew out of resourcefulness rather than primary materials; in Murcia, the silk industry and mines were thriving again, but agriculture was held back by the aridity of many areas. The two regions shared many problems: plague epidemics decimated the pop-

Top: typical Muslim terracing near Pego
Above: a fine example of Arab influence

ulation in the 17th century; and Berber piracy led to a fear of invasion
and the building of watchtowers and fortresses on the coast (as at Santa
Pola and Campello).

A further serious blow was the expulsion of the *moriscos,* the Muslims
who had stayed after the Reconquest and provided an invaluable skilled
workforce. At first their customs and language were tolerated, but from the
early 16th century they became a scapegoat for economic problems. Growing
enmity found ritual voice in forced conversions and, finally, in expulsion
in 1609 by Philip III. Initially, the Murcian *moriscos* were exempted because
of their importance to the economy, but a few years later they, too, were
expelled. A long economic and cultural recession resulted and the region
did not recover fully till the 18th century.

Shaping a Spanish Identity

With the drawn-out War of Succession of 1702–14 and the accession to the
throne of Philip V – the first of the Bourbon monarchs – the political map
was redrawn. Many cities and towns in Valencia, which had backed Charles,
Archduke of Austria, lost their rights. In contrast, areas that had solidly
supported the Bourbon cause, such as Murcia and Alicante, benefited from
royal favour. In the century that followed, the economic potential of many
areas began to be realised for the first time since the Reconquest. Reservoirs,
windmills and aqueducts were built to irrigate arid areas; forests were cleared
to plant vines, olives and cereals; the lower Segura valley was drained to
become fertile *huerta.* Workshops producing silk and other textiles flourished
in both Murcia and Alicante, and, in the middle of the century, industrial techniques appeared in Alcoi. Public works programmes and Genoese traders
helped the ports to develop; Cartagena became a major defensive arsenal;
Alicante boasted Spain's third-largest volume of trade.

The region's new wealth and confidence was expressed in a massive
building boom that incorporated a late flowering of baroque architec-

Above: the marriage of Ferdinand and Isabella unified Aragon and Castile

ture. Palaces and señorial houses acquired ornate façades; churches were topped by blue-tiled cupolas like teapot lids; Murcia, Lorca and Orihuela were remodelled. The decorative flair – which also found expression in fiestas and costumes – represented a dynamic society with a growing influence from Castile.

Anarchists and Secessionists

The creation of a new middle class continued through the 19th century. Progress was checked temporarily by the War of Independence against the French and an earthquake in the Segura valley, but it was quickened by the confiscation and redistribution of monastery estates. The provincial boundaries of the 1830s marked the beginning of Orihuela's decline and Alicante's rise as a local capital. Improved transport brought new markets for agricultural produce and the first tourists, while industrialisation in Alcoi and Cartagena brought in new political ideas. During the first Republic of 1873, anarchist workers at Alcoi seized the town, killed the mayor and the Guardia Civil, while at Cartagena, cantonalists seeking regional secession introduced divorce and abolished the death penalty before being bombarded into submission. Mining wealth left its mark in some wonderful Modernist architecture at Cartagena, Jumilla, Alcoi, La Unión and Novelda, where there is a small museum.

For all this, rural 19th-century life – uninterrupted by invasion, immigration or cultural exchange – maintained a local quality. The vineyard regions around Monóvar, Dénia, Yecla and Jumilla boomed briefly when phylloxera destroyed French vines; the poor fishing and smuggling villages, such as Benidorm or Torrevieja; the green *huerta* of the Segura valley, its adobe *barracas* periodically swept away by flooding; the harsh northern valleys, where life still centred on the old *morisco* hamlets; the southern Campo de Cartagena, where windmills drew up water and ground wheat. All these geographical pockets lived as worlds apart from one another.

As they became sucked into the international marketplace, they suffered economically. At the turn of the century, vineyards and olive groves were torn up to make way for citrus fruit and almonds. The poverty never became as desperate as that of the south – the wealth of the *huertas* and the shared inheritance system meant there were more property owners than labourers – but the flow of emigration to local cities, North Africa and Catalunya was steady and, in the bad years of the early 1930s, it rose to a flood.

When civil war broke out in 1936, Murcia and the Levante (eastern Spain) declared for Republicanism and sent brigades to the military fronts. At home, churches were looted, cities bombarded. The collectivisation of land followed apace. After the fall of Madrid and the Republican government in Valencia, the region fell to the Nationalists in 1939.

Right: church domes in Jijona

Tourism and New Horizons

The postwar decade under Franco's military dictatorship saw painfully slow reconstruction by an exhausted country. Not until the 1950s did the economy strengthen and the gap close between town and country, inland and coastal areas. Driving here in the late 1940s, the British writer Rose Macaulay observed, 'This is a haunted shore: ghosts around each bay, each little town, each castled rock, whispering in the lap of waves and in the low rumour of the sea wind in the palms.'

Just a decade later, the tourist invasion was underway. The first real boom took place in the 1960s: skyscrapers replaced the old *ventas* (inns) and the number of visitors to Alicante province shot up to over 3 million a year. Smaller but significant booms followed in the 1970s and 1980s, spreading down the coast to the Mar Menor and inland to the valleys and sierras. Apart from tourism's often disastrous impact on the coastal landscape and its huge boost to the local economy, tourism became a cultural phenomenon in the 1960s, bringing in its wake social liberalisation and a new bourgeoisie long before Franco's death and the arrival of democracy in 1978.

Industry and agriculture have survived. Industry, some of it still based on traditional local crafts, provides work for more than a quarter of the population, and vineyards and fruit groves flourish. The emergence of a strong regional culture – language, fiestas, cooking, dance, crafts and music – has occurred alongside the dawn of a new electronic and hi-tech economy. Film studios and theme parks are springing up along the coast.

At the same time the scale of tourism is putting huge pressure on the environment. Today, for example, there are more hotel beds in Benidorm than Greece, and Torrevieja plays host to half a million visitors in the summer months. Falling catches of fish, mountain fires, soil and beach erosion and dramatic water shortages have highlighted the fragility of ecological balance here. A new awareness of the need to protect countryside, control heavy industry, to treat water as a precious resource and to restrict development will influence the Costa's history in the next decade.

Meanwhile, the relaxed Mediterranean lifestyle remains. That, together with the high average incomes here and the newly cosmopolitan, multilingual society, has helped to create an arc of affluence that already represents the future integrated Europe of which many politicians dream.

HISTORY HIGHLIGHTS

c50,000BC First evidence of cave dwellings (found in Cueva del Cochino, Villena; Cueva de las Calaveres, Benidoleig).

8th century BC Phoenician traders introduce the pottery wheel, the fig and the olive.

23 AD Quart Hades founded on site of Cartagena.

218–19 Roman army, under Publio Cornelio Scipio, conquers Spanish Mediterranean coast, from Emporias to the Carthaginian capital, Quart Hades, which they rename Cartago Nova.

AD555 Byzantine troops conquer Cartago, but lose all their territory to Visigoths by 624.

711–14 Muslims invade and conquer Iberian peninsula, except for areas in the northwest.

756 Caliphate of Córdoba founded.

1010–95 Taifa kingdoms in power (in this area, Dénia and Murcia).

1095 Almoravides, Berbers from the Atlas mountains, invade.

1160 Another Berber tribe, the Almohades, invade.

13th century The Reconquest moves southwards in a two-pronged drive by Castile and Aragon.

1243–4 Kingdom of Murcia ceded by Ben-Hud dynasty to Castile.

1238–48 James I of Aragon conquers northern Alicante.

1263 Muslim rebellion in Murcia is put down by James I of Aragon.

1276 Muslim revolt in Alicante finally quashed.

1304 The Treaty of Torrellas confirms Alicante's annexation of Castilian territory south to Mar Menor.

1361 Pedro the Cruel finally captures Alicante for Castile after repeated attempts. (His brother, Henry II of Trastamara, later returns it after Pedro's death.)

1474 Ferdinand and Isabella marry to unite Castile and Aragon.

1492 Fall of Muslim Granada. The expulsion of Spanish Jews.

1519 Revolt against nobility and persecution of *moriscos* (converted Muslims) in the kingdom of Valencia.

1609 Expulsion of *moriscos*.

1702–14 Spanish War of Succession between Philip of Anjou (V) and Charles, Duke of Hapsburg.

1783 Death of Francisco Salzillo, baroque sculptor.

1808–12 War of Independence (also known as the Peninsular War) against the French.

1812 A Spanish constitution written.

1829 Earthquake destroys towns of Lower Segura valley.

1833–6 Present provincial borders are fixed: Villena, Dénia and Orihuela are included in Alicante province.

1858 The Alicante–Madrid railway line opens.

1862 Railway line from Madrid to Murcia city opens.

1873 First Republic: *cantanolismo* (secession) in Cartagena.

1888 In Cartagena, Isaac Peral builds what is claimed to be the world's first working submarine.

1936–9 Civil War: Alicante and Murcia remain Republican.

1939 Surrender to the Nationalists after fall of Madrid.

1960–71 The number of visitors annually to Alicante province rises from 950,000 to more than 3,750,000.

1982 Statutes of Autonomy of Valencia and Murcia regions (Alicante becomes Valencia's southern province).

1992 Spain becomes a full member state of the European Union.

2000 The population of Alicante city reaches 1,445,000, double that of 1960.

Left: sun, sand and sea at Benidorm

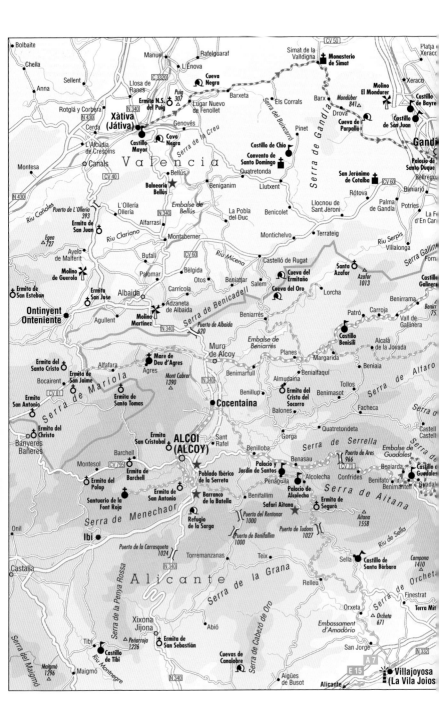

ATJA DE XERESA

PLATJA DE EL GRAO DE GANDIA

PLATJA DE GANDÍA

atja de Gandía
PLATJA DE VENECIA

Platja de Bellreguard
Platja Miramar
Platja de Piles
Piles   PLATJA DE OLIVA

Oliva   Platja d'Olives
Castillo de los
Duques de Gandia
A 7

E 15
San Pedro

Northern Costa Blanca
10 km / 6 miles

Itinerary 1
Itinerary 2
Itinerary 3
Itinerary 4
Itinerary 5
Itinerary 6

M a r   M e d i t e r r á n e o
(M e d i t e r r a n e a n   S e a)

PLATJA DE VERGEL
Punta de los Molinos

subia   Safari   CV 715   CV 730
Pego   Ermita de   Miraflor   **Dénia**   PLATJA DE DENIA
stillo   San Sebastián   Vergel   Torre de Cero
misera   Ráfol de   Ondara   CV 7222   La Xara   Les Arenetes
Cora   Almunia   Las Rotas   Cueva de Agua Dulce
del Rull   Beniarbeig   Ermita de   CV 736
all de Ebo   Sagra   Río Girona   San Juan   Cap de Sant Antoni
Embalse   Benidoleig   Poblado   △ 755   Aduanas del Mar
de Isbert   Pedreguer   Ibérico   Montgó
himaurell   Orba   Cueva de las   N 332   Jesús   **XÀBIA**   PLATJA ARENA
Vall de   Castillo   Calaveras   Pobre   **(JÁVEA)**   Cala
Laguart   de Orba   Camacho   CV 734   Blanca   *Cap de Sant Martin*
Benichembla   Gata de   I. de Portitxol
CV 715   Alcalalí   Gorgos   Río Gorgos   Rafalet   Cueva des Orguens
coll   Parcent   Lliber   La Garganta   El Tosalet   Cap de la Nau
047   Col de Rates   Xaló   (Desfiladero)   La Granadella
rrascal de Parcent   80   (Jalón)   Senija   Benitachell   PLATJA DE LA GRANADELLA
astillo de   Teulada   CALA DE LOS TIESTOS
Bolulla   Castillo de   Benissa   Benimarco   Cumbre   PLATJA DE CUMBRE DEL SOL
Tárbena   los Moros   N 332   del Sol
El Pinós   Buena Vista   El Portet de Morella
ixorta   Punta de Moraira
Callosa d'En   Ermita del   PLATJA DE MORAIRA
Sarrià   Fonts   Bernia   Vicario   Calp   PLATJA DE LEVANTE
de Algar   1129   Burranco de   (Calpe)   Peñón d'Ifac
Ermita de   Altea   Mascarat   Ruinas de Calpe
San Lorenzo   la Vieja   Peñón de Ifach
lón   CV 755   (Penyal d'Ifac)
a Nucia   Olla de Altea   PLATJA DEL
El Tosal   PUERTO
Rafael   **Altea**
CV 70   Alfa del Pi
arrina   Platja   Punta Bombarda
Aqualandia   de Albir
Rincón de Loix
BENIDORM
Punta de l'Escaleta
PLATJA DE LEVANTE
ATJA LA CALA

C o s t a   B l a n c a

Serra de Segaría

Serra del Montgó

Serra del Ferrer

Río Guadalest

The North

1. EXPLORING THE NORTHERN COAST: CALPE TO THE COL DE RATES *(see map, p18–19)*

Allow 4 hours for the Peñón d'Ifach (a rocky coastal outcrop), the small town of Benissa and a beach. A leisurely drive (2½ hours with stops) loops back into wine country and up to a sierra viewpoint before dining at a country restaurant.

Dotted around the coastline of northern Alicante province, between the up-market family resorts and the ribbon of villas running between them, are unspoiled pockets with areas of lovely countryside. The towns and villages carry reminders of a long history of piracy and invasion. Start at **Calpe** (Calp), dubbed 'Muy Heroica Villa' by Charles V for its stoic defence against Berber pirates. Just outside the town, now a busy resort, is the **Peñón d'Ifach** (Penyal d'Ifac in Catalan). a huge limestone fang rearing out of the sea charted by ancient mariners and later used as a watchtower against pirates. It is now a symbol for the Costa Blanca, overlooking crowded beaches on either side but still keeping its splendid isolation.

The easiest parking place is in the fishing port below. From there it is a long climb up – the Peñón is 330m (1,083ft) high – through a tunnel in the bottom of the rock face (allow 30–40 mins). It is worth the effort though, since the views over the coastline are superb. The slopes and rocky bays below are worth clambering over too; they are now a *parque natural* protecting over 300 plant species – including a unique orchid and carnation – which grow in the sheltered micro-climate. In summer, it is a good idea to start early, since the number of visitors is limited, and visit the study centre afterwards. There is also a shady picnic area nearby.

From the Peñón, cut back inland to **Benissa**, a town built several miles inland for safety from pirate attacks, with *rejas* (iron grills) over the windows. Everything of interest here is in one, long narrow strip running from the top to the bottom of the town. At the very top, in Calle Escoto, the Franciscan **Convento de los Capuchinos**, founded in 1611, is built of soft golden stone (ring on the doorbell to visit). Lower down, in the centre of town, the **Calle de la Purísima** is lined with lovely old medieval houses, often with old porches and gable designs of Muslim origin, and the 15th-century agricultural exchange houses a **Museu de Etnografía**, due to reopen in 2004 after years of restoration. Opposite you can pick up a late breakfast or mid-morning snack at a knock-out bakery, **Bolufer**.

Make your way back to the coast via Teulada and Benitachell, where smaller roads and tracks run down

Left: the Peñón d'Ifach rears out of the sea at Calpe
Right: a Costa Blanca letter box personified

past holiday housing to the beaches around the **Cap de la Nau** and **Cap de Sant Antoni**. The most spectacular of these is the Cala de Moraig, an enclosed golden strip sheltered by tall cliffs reached through the Cumbre del Sol estate, considered an environmental crime by many local people. Less abrasive are **Platja de la Granadella**, further round, or the **Platja de Mar Azul**, looking over the tiny Isla de Portixol. It has good snorkelling, a diving pontoon and a couple of breezy beach bars.

Xàbia to the Gorgos Valley

Outside beach weather, it is easy to while away an hour or two in **Xàbia** (**Jávea**). The town has a fine fortified Gothic church, its tawny stones softened and pockmarked by the salt winds. Nearby is the **Museo Arqueológico y Etnográfico** (Calle Primicias 1; Tues–Sun Nov–Feb 10am–1pm; Mar–Oct 10am–1pm and 6–8pm; July and Aug until 11pm; entrance fee), which explores the history of the coast from Palaeolithic caves and Iberian villages to Roman wealth and medieval poverty. It also has an excellent collection of Muslim ceramics and craft equipment, such as *alpargata* tools and a raisin press.

From here, it is a short coastal drive west past the deserted terraces of the **Serra del Montgó**, now a Natural Park, to the fish restaurants of **Dénia**. (As you come down into the bay take a sharp right, marked for Les Rotes, and then look for signs.) They are famed for their *arroz abanda*, rice cooked in a rich fish stock flavoured with saffron and sautéed tomato and onion. It may look plain next to most tourist *paellas*, but the flavour is wonderful. **El Pegolí**, one of several such restaurants, is particularly memorable *(see page 76)*. From here you can walk out to the shoreline for a siesta or drive down to to **Les Roques**, the old fishing quarter, where the day's catch is auctioned at 5pm *(for more on Dénia see page 26)*.

the north

Alternatively, an afternoon drive can loop back into the olive and citrus groves, stopping off quickly for a glimpse of **Ondara's** wonderful small bullring, which sits on the northern edge of the town. Access is through the Bar Plaça de Bous: tickets for the fights, as well as concerts in summer, sell fast and need to be bought well in advance.

A short drive further on, at **Gata de Gorgos**, you turn off to **Llíber**, driving through rolling hills into the well-tamed wine country of the **Gorgos Valley**. As you approach **Xaló (Jalón)**, the soil turns from red to yellow and vineyards begin to cover the valley floor. They were once famed for their sweet malmsey and raisins made from muscatel grapes. Today the vineyards are still dotted by the characteristic *riu-raus*, arched porches used for drying the grapes, but they are hardly used. Xaló itself is a tranquil town dominated by a vast 19th-century church, with a good wine cooperative where you can taste and buy the claret-like red and excellent sweet muscatel wines (*see page 72*). From here, drive on up to the **Col de Rates** – signposted for Tárbena and Callosa – a bare lookout point (780m/2,559ft) with great views.

Immediately below is **Parcent**, a dozy village where life rotates around the agricultural cooperative and its splendid *fin-de-siglo* bar. Stop off here for a local wine or *mosto* – unfermented grape juice – before backtracking towards the coast for a special dinner at La Seu (*see page 77*), close to Teulada.

2. THE NORTHERN HILL TOWNS
AND SERRA DE AITANA *(see map, p18–19)*

A 1½ hour drive from the lush coast behind Benidorm takes you past a waterfall and hill villages to two historic inland towns: Cocentaina and Alcoi. To see everything along the way, you need to make an early start or, for a leisurely day, make a choice of destinations before you start. The drive back crosses the Serra de Aitana, with spectacular views.

In the northern sierras, all roads seem to lead to **Alcoi (Alcoy)**. Sited in a sheltered river plain where a number of rivers converge behind the coastal hills, it is both the oldest and largest of the northern hill towns, the old town looking down on textile and paper factories which grew out of Moorish workshops.

A first stop can be made at the **Fonts de Algar** (*see page 29*), freshwater pools just outside **Callosa d'En Sarriá**. The road then runs on to Alcoi past Guadalest and Confrides, the lush vegetation dropping away together with the subtropical micro-climate as the road winds up between harsh sierras to the chalky plateau of Alcoi. Just after Benilloba, take the right turn to **Cocentaina** (20 mins).

Above Left: the steep slope of Benissa. **Left:** rooftops in Xàbia
Right: faces of the future in Alcoi

Cocentaina

One of the most beautiful small towns of the province, Cocentaina has clearly delineated medieval Christian and Jewish quarters on either side of the **Palau Comtal**, a 15th- to 16th-century fortified palace. After years of restoration, the palace is now open to the public (Mon–Sat 10.30am–1.30pm, tel: 965-590159 to check; informal guided tour, 30 mins, no charge). In the

chapel hangs the *Mare de Déu*, a painting of the Virgin Mary said to have miraculously burst into tears. Elsewhere some rooms have fine wooden ceilings and tiled floors, fragments of the former magnificence of the palace. The **Sala Dorada**, the Palau Comtal's most richly decorated room, situated on its western corner, is dedicated to the wartime victories of the Aragonese crown. The neighbouring **Convento de Clarisas** (7am–noon and evening Mass) is also worth a quick peek inside for its collection of fine paintings, which include a 15th-century Byzantine *retablo*.

The old quarter comes to life for the Fira de Tots Sants – All Saints' Day Fair – the oldest of its kind in Spain (celebrated since 1346), which combines the best of an agricultural and medieval fair and draws large crowds.

For good eating, drive a short way outside town to La Escaleta, an excellent Michelin-starred restaurant. An alternative is a picnic in the **Font Roja** natural park, a 20-minute drive on the other side of Alcoi. The 19th-century chapel is superbly sited next to an icy water source. From here, paths lead up into beautiful Mediterranean woodland with *carrascas* (kermes oaks), which are now a protected species.

Alcoi

Late afternoon, when the streets are coming back to life, is the perfect time to arrive in **Alcoi**. As you approach from Cocentaina over the suspension bridge, the town's geography is at its most dramatic, with houses appearing to topple down into a gorge cut by the meeting of rivers. The town centre is quite distinct from others in the province, with architectural character thanks to its early industrialisation: hence the old-fashioned banks and shops (for example in **Calle Juan Cantó**), the frilly modernist balconies and workers' cultural centres, the five bridges and the 19th-century cotton factories, now restored into modern office spaces.

The open spaces are thoroughly 19th-century too. La Bandeja, as the main Plaça d'Espanya is known, is heavy and grandiose; but the smaller

Above: doves flutter in Alcoi's Plaça de Dins

neighbouring **Plaça de Dins**, where doves flutter around over the site of the convent torn down in the 1820s, and the nearby **Glorieta**, a park with peacocks and a tall dovecote, are charming places to observe well-dressed provincial Spanish life.

Below the main square is the graceful old core of the town. The 17th-century town hall houses the local archaeological museum; **Museu Arqueologic Municipal** (Mon–Fri 9am–2pm, Sat, Sun and holidays 10.30am–1.30pm; closed weekends July–Aug), whose exhibits include the local equivalent of the Rosetta stone: a small lead tablet with writing in an undeciphered Iberian alphabet and the Iberian Dama de Jerreta.

Nearby is the **Museu de Festes**, the private museum of the town's hedonistic Moors and Christians fiesta (C. San Miguel 60, Tues–Fri 11am–1pm and 5.30–7.30pm, weekends and holidays 10.30am–1.30pm; entrance fee). The pomp of the costumes and the paraphernalia that goes with them is extraordinary, as is their expense; to the people of Alcoi, the fiestas are a matter of great pride.

A Romantic Garden

To return to the coast, take the mountain road over the **Sierra de Aitana** via the villages of Benifallim and **Penaguila**, where you can visit the lovely **Jardin de Santos** (Apr–Sept Wed–Sun 11am–6.45pm, 8.45pm weekends; Oct–Mar Wed–Sun 10.30am–4.15pm, 5.15pm weekends). From here there is a slow but beautiful road over the mountains to the coast via **Relleu**, a lovely unspoilt village from which you can walk to an Arab castle. There are paths up into the mountains, semi-alpine flora and some fine views here, plus bars where you can have a drink while watching the sun set.

The trip could be stretched into a two-day excursion by adding on a day to walk in the new National Park of the Serra de Mariola *(see page 28)*.

Above: Spain's most famous Moors and Christians fiesta in Alcoi

3. DÉNIA AND THE TRAIN SOUTH *(see map, p18–19)*

After exploring the pleasant town of Dénia, enjoy a relaxing train ride south to Alicante. Train details are on page 92.

Dénia's elegant air of old wealth makes it quite distinct from other resorts. 'Of all the lovely places down the Iberian seaboard, I believe Dénia…to be the most attractive,' remarked the British writer and traveller Rose Macaulay when she visited the town in 1949. Perhaps it appealed to her so much because of the English colonial imprint left by raisin dealers who lived here from 1800 to the Civil War. The large, sweet raisins are still renowned for their quality (the Monday street-market by the station or the municipal market in Calle Carlos Senti are the best places to buy raisins) and one of the raisin warehouses stands on Calle Mar.

Five minutes' walk from the station are the shady main avenue and **Plaza de la Constitución**, where the 17th-century church (open during Mass) faces the *ayuntamiento*, tumbling with bougainvillaea and geraniums in summer. Inlaid in its Renaissance façade is a stone from the Roman **Temple of Diana** after which the town itself was named – the inhabitants of Dénia are still called *dianenses*.

Other monuments are the walls and towers of the **castle**, one of the most important of the Mediterranean coast, which was built by the troops during the siege of the Muslim town and refortified during the War of Independence, when the French occupied the town for four years. Underneath runs a long tunnel cut through the rock, and inside is a small **archaeological museum** (the daily opening times vary: 10am–1.30pm and 5–7.30pm in July–Aug, for example). Close by, the small **Museo Etnologico** (Calle Cavellers s/n; Tues–Sat 10.30am–1pm and 4–7pm, Sun am only)

Above: the Museo Etnologico in Dénia. **Left:** Cervantes landed in Dénia on his return from Algiers

has old photos of raisin-making, work tools and furniture. Another curiosity, found along the walk between the city centre beach, **Les Rotes** and the seafood restaurants, is the English cemetery, where raisin merchants and sailors were buried. The walk to Les Rotes takes 25 minutes in all, bringing you to a series of idyllically quiet, small rocky coves.

The Trenet

From Dénia you can travel on the Trenet, or single-track train, which runs south to Campello, where it connects with a tram service to **Alicante**. It is an endearing hangover from the past, for an express train it is not: it makes 43 stops on a 50-mile journey taking 2½ hours.

This is its great advantage, for you can reach many parts of the coast (and the countryside behind it) without getting bogged down in traffic and, at the same time, enjoy the scenery and watch the local passengers going about their daily business. You can also take your bicycle with you for only a few extra cents. Currently trains leave every two hours between 5.50am and 6.50pm. At weekends special tickets combine a train ride with a guided walk from one of the stations along the route.

The most scenic stretch is between **Dénia** and **Calp**, initially passing through lush citrus groves but soon entering the dry lands behind the coastal plain. Ferrandet and Xara (Jara) stations give access to hilly walking country in the Serras de Montgó and Bérnia. The views here have changed less than you might expect since Rose Macaulay followed the same route by road in 1949, 'through strange ash-pale country, very dry, with little vines and olives, and huge, odd-shaped rocks and mountains'. Further south is Benidorm's futuristic skyline, also worth watching out for.

4. THE GALLINERA VALLEY: MORISCO VILLAGES AND CHERRY BLOSSOM *(see map, p18–19)*

The inland valley between Pego and Agres (total 1½ hours' drive without stopping), and the smaller Alcalà and Ebo valleys running off it, can be seen in a day, although a longer stay will be rewarding.

Nowhere is the contrast between the modernity of the coast and the traditional way of life inland so marked as it is in the **Vall de Gallinera** with its quiet agricultural villages, Muslim imprint and surrounding sierras. To get a proper feel for this region allow two to three days, leaving time to walk as well as drive. The springboard for the area is **Pego**, a bustling small town which has lost its rice fields but keeps the local architecture of farm villages. If the church is open for morning mass (9–10am) you will be able to see the fine 15th-century *retablo* of the pregnant **Virgen de la Esperanza** inside.

Right: life in the slow lane

From Pego, take the road to Planes (marked for **Muro de Alcoy** or **Muro del Comtat**) which follows the Vall de Gallinera. The traces of the converted Muslims who stayed after the Reconquest quickly show themselves: the terracing of the steeply banked hillsides, and then, after the road has run through a spectacular gorge, the Arabic names and layout of the old *alquerías*, or hamlets. Some of the more isolated villages – **Alcalà de la Jovada**, for example – even have deserted, dry-stone *morisco* ruins still standing. The area became a stronghold for rebellion: one revolt, led by the charismatic Al-Azraq, lasted from 1258–75; another was a dramatic last stand by 15,000 *moriscos* against expulsion in 1609. Outnumbered, they eventually surrendered and were deported from Dénia the following spring.

Just before Planes, a track hairpinning down to the right signed for the **Barranc del' Encanta** ('enchanted ravine') leads to a wonderful blue swimming hole fed by a waterfall. From here you can walk along the valley between olive and citrus groves, or drive on up to the ruined castle at **Lorcha**.

Perched on a small hill below a ruined 12th-century castle, **Planes** keeps its medieval shape, a 17th-century aqueduct built for a long defunct distillery, the oldest fiesta in the province (*see page 84*) and a string of bars along the main road.

The Serra de Mariola

It is only half-an-hour's drive west from here to **Agres**, tucked into the side of its quiet valley. The **Pensión Mariola** (*see page 94*) makes a comfortable, quiet rural base for the walking country in the **Serra de Mariola**, the region's newest Natural Park. There are medieval snow-wells in which ice was made for use in summer, prehistoric caves and a large number of wild herbs (take the forest path up past the sanctuary, which is also worth a look). Down in the valley, a path leads along various stretches of the river and there is an old *balneario* or spa. A short drive on up the valley will also bring you to **Bocairent**, a quiet market town with a picturesque medieval quarter and a bullring carved into the rock.

An alternative route for your return journey takes you along the road to Alcalà de la Jovada through the **Vall d'Ebo** and past the **Cova del Rull**, a cave full of spectacular stalactites and stalagmites (Apr–Sept 10.30am–8pm; Nov–Feb 11am–5pm, Oct and Mar closes 6.30pm). The valley's cherry blossom is a wonderful sight in April and May and the Vall d'Ebo cooperative sells the cherries in season, varietal honeys, almonds and olive oil. On the final stretch to Pego, the road passes the spectacular Barranc del Infiern (literally Hell Gorge), accessible only to skilled climbers, then drops to the coast with splendid views along the way.

After all this, returning to the coast comes as a shock. One is left wondering how long the valleys can resist the development creeping up from the resorts.

Above: a medieval snow-well on the slopes of the Serra de Mariola

5. THE GUADALEST VALLEY AND ALTEA
(see map, p18–19)

Allow 45 minutes driving time to Guadalest from the turn-off behind Benidorm, and the same to Altea. En route you will find a spectacular waterfall, a Muslim castle with panoramic views and lush medlar groves.

The **Guadalest Valley** is one of the most photogenic of Alicante province's landscapes, with tall peaks and hill villages above lush green valleys. Start in **Polop de la Marina**, a sleepy village with the tall mountain of **Ponoch** looming above it on one side. The main sight here is the Font Els Zorros, a modern extension of the old water fountain with 221 spouts. From here the village streets slope steeply up towards the deserted cemetery, built on the site of the ruined castle. There are fine views over the valley floor below and the surrounding peaks, often backed by swirling clouds.

The road continues to Callosa d'En Sarrià, where you turn off to the **Fonts de Algar** waterfalls (take the road to Tárbena and follow the signs; there is a large car park). Buried in a jungly-green valley filled with citrus and medlar groves, the water alternates between cascades and pools, running between river banks covered with pink oleander and bougainvillaea in summer. Starting at the lowest and most spectacular waterfall and natural bathing pool, you can climb up alongside the river for 20 minutes or so until it becomes a mountain stream and then, where the path runs out, wade on up to the top (open 10am–7pm; entrance fee).

Up to the Castle

Return to Callosa and take the turning for **Benimantell**, which runs through loquat, almond and olive groves and gives you the best first view of the village of **Guadalest**, its castle and bell tower precariously balanced on fangs of rock rearing up from the valley. This was one of the Muslim network of castles which collected taxes and kept an eye on the scattered rural hamlets

Above: the Guadalest castle overlooking its reservoir

in these northern valleys. Now, the silhouette and view from the top of the castle are, in truth, its best points since the handful of streets are overrun with souvenir stalls and there is little to see except for the entrance arch to the town and the 12th-century dungeon. There is a small private museum of rural life here, the **Museo Etnológico** (10am–6pm, later in summer; closed Sat in winter), which recreates a late 19th-century farmhouse.

From here you can drive down through the neighbouring village of **Beniardá** and round the reservoir to the dam, before climbing up to the main road again. It is then half an hour's drive back to Callosa, winding round between groves of loquats and citrus trees, and dropping down to cross the river. In summer, oleander, bougainvillaea and purple convolvulus tumble around the roadside in glorious profusion.

From Callosa it is a short but winding drive down to **Altea la Vieja** (or **La Vella**), identifiable by its blue church dome. Carefully restored by the colony of artists who moved in during the 1950s, it is now hoping to become a miniature cultural capital thanks to the arrival of a new arts university, a major new concert hall, the **Palau** (C. Alcoy s/n), with an exhibition of musical instruments from around the world (open Mon–Sat 10am–2pm and 5–8pm), and, outside town, the **Centro Internacional de la Musica Villa Gadea** (Pda la Olla 26), set up by UNESCO as a home for five international music foundations. The centre has beautiful gardens running down to the pebbly beach. The café *terrazas* in the old town's attractive plaza are busy in the evening, with a good variety to choose from. **La Capella** (*see page 75 for details*) is a good choice for well prepared traditional dishes.

6. THE LAND OF THE BORJAS: XÀTIVA AND GANDIA
(see map, p18–19)

A 40-minute drive north from the coast is Xàtiva, the home town of the famous Borja family. Allow 2–3 hours to look around. On your return to the coast stop off at Gandía to see its interesting archaeological museum and the Palacio de Santo Duque.

The spectacular saga of the Borja family (also spelt Borgia), legendary for its nepotism, power politics and sexual intrigues, is usually associated with Rome. From there Alfonso de Borja, Pope Calixto III, orchestrated the 15th-century campaign against the Turks, his nephew Alexander VI carved up

Above: a cool spot for a drink on Altea's Plaza de la Iglesia

the New World between the Spanish and Portuguese and his son, Caesar, on whom Machiavelli modelled *The Prince*, conspired to have his brother murdered. But the Borjas were of Spanish blood, with their family home in the Valencian hill town of Xàtiva (Játiva in *castellano*) and their aristocratic base in the nearby duchy of Gandía.

Historic Xàtiva

Xàtiva, a pleasant 40-minute drive back from the coast, is the more interesting of the two towns. Try to visit it on Tuesday or Thursday when you can see the bustling market; otherwise, make sure you come when the **Museo del Almudira** is open (Tues–Sun 10am–2pm, Oct–Mar also 4–6pm). Its small but interesting collection traces the town's growth from Roman *castrum* (fortress), Visigothic bishopric and cultivated Arab town – thought to be one of the first places where paper was made in Europe – to royal city from the 14th to the 17th centuries. The collection includes a unique Romanesque font, and paintings by José Ribera (d.1591), nicknamed El Spagnaletto, yet another famous native son who made his name in Italy.

To make sure you catch everything of interest in the old town, follow the tourist office's numbered walking route, which takes you past old palaces, noble houses – including Alexander VI's birthplace – fountains and churches to **La Seo**, the huge collegiate church, which was sacked in the Civil War (Mon–Sat 10.30am–1pm). On the top of the hill above are the **ruins** (Tues–Sun 10am–7pm; Oct–Mar closes at 6pm; allow an hour) of the Roman to medieval city and castle, destroyed by Philip III in revenge for Xàtiva's siding against him in the War of Succession, and, just below that, the 13th-century church of **San Feliu** (open Tue–Sun 10am–1pm, 4–7pm, 3–6pm Oct–Mar), its doorway built with columns from the Roman Temple on the same site. For lunch, *see page 76.*

Palace of the Borjas

Gandía cannot compare with Xàtiva for atmosphere or monumental wealth, but it does have an excellent new **archaeological museum** inside a 14th-century hospital, a **collegiate church** built in the time of of Calixtus III (open for Mass Mon–Sat 11.30am, 7.30pm, Sun also 10.30am, 8.30pm) and the sumptuous 16th- to 18th-century former palace of the Borjas, the **Palacio de Santo Duque** (Mon–Fri, guided tours 11am and 6pm; 11am and 5pm in winter), which was turned into Spain's first Jesuit college by the fourth duke, Francisco Borja who, as a widower, became the Superior of the order. The palace has an outstanding allegorical tiled floor. Nearby is a good cake-shop, **Dolços Toni**, Calle Pares Jesuits 5, where you can recover from so much religiosity

Right: outside the San Feliu church in Xàtiva

7. A Night on the Town: Benidorm and Terra Mitica

(see map opposite)

You'll need your own car or a taxi to get from the old town to the clubs off Levante beach. In summer, you can take a ride on the coastal night train, the Trensnochador, which runs through from 9pm to 5am and stops at Terra Mítica, Europe's largest theme park. Buses run there from Benidorm.

It is easy to knock **Benidorm** – particularly when you have never set eyes on the place. Most people who have actually been there will admit that it has a fascination akin to that of Las Vegas. One of the largest resorts in the world, with as many hotel bedrooms as Greece, it is a huge fun factory dominated by the 52-storey Hotel Bali. And, quite apart from all this, its nightlife has something to offer everyone, from a bosanova or garage fan to an 80-year-old granny.

Arrive at sundown as the three miles of white sand are emptying, and you will be in time to catch the evening *paseo*. Follow the signs through the mini-skyscrapers to the **Playa** (or **Platja**) **de Levante** (if you are in a car, leave it in the underground park off Avda de L'Aigüera) and stroll along the front, past the tea cafés where senior citizens happily tango away winter afternoons. Despite all the foreigners, the *paseo* is also a wonderful cross-section of old and new Spain: mini-skirted girls twice the height of their grand-mothers, old men in their berets, women gesticulating with their fans. Later, around midnight, the bars pack out with young Spaniards.

The broad expanse of white sand, around which Benidorm grew from a tiny fishing village to a giant resort in only fifty years, is an object lesson in how beaches can be kept clean if you really try. An army of rubbish collectors move in at dusk, and after midnight dumper trucks start sifting out cigarette butts and oxygenating the sand. Out in the bay, a filter cleans and monitors the water. Beach bars are banned. Hence, despite the 45,000 people who squeeze onto the twin beaches at the height of the season, the sands have been declared among the cleanest in the world.

Once it is dark, walk back to **L'Aigüera** park (dawn–10pm; July–Sept to 1am), designed by Catalan architect Ricardo Bofill and the first major piece

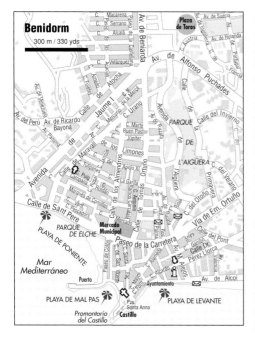

of public architecture in one of the coastal resorts. Built along a dry river valley, its central avenue runs up through sweeping classical perspectives which are transformed at night by blue and white neon lighting. The new town hall in front of the park – also designed by Bofill – is a grandiose monument to the profits of tourism.

Eating options break the mould since Benidorm is now a year-round Spanish residential town. For addresses, see *page 75* – or pick up a snack in the old town. There are a good range of tapas bars on C. Santo Domingo.

Theme Parks and Nightclubs

Alternatively, if you've decided on a trip to **Terra Mítica** (Camino de Moralet s/n; opens at 10am all year round; closing times vary betwen 6pm and midnight; tel: 902 020 220 for details; reduced entrance fee for children under 12 and OAPs, and in winter), Europe's largest theme park covering 105 hectares, you can eat in one of the 80 restaurants there. The park – 3km (2 miles) inland from Benidorm – takes the Mediterranean classical civilisations as its theme; rides include the Magnus Colossus, the largest wooden rollercoaster in Europe. Critics says the technology cannot compare to Port Aventura, the theme park at Salou on the Costa Dorada, but the food and shops gain by turning their back on Americana as decisively as the rides. A sister theme park, **Terra Natura**, with wildlife from around the world, is scheduled to open next door in 2004.

Back in Benidorm itself are two main centres of nightlife. The first is the old town, where you will find a more native atmosphere in local bars, ice cream parlours and *horchaterías* as well as the gay clubs, which are thick on the ground here. These usually have a relaxed, mixed clientele. The other main area is new Benidorm, further towards the edge of town on the Avenida de la Comunitat Valenciano at the far end of the **Levante beach**, where **Penélope** – the biggest disco – and its rivals are clustered together. More interesting in this zone are **L'Anouer** or **Ku**, ta futuristic discotheque, or **Conuco**, a lively salsa joint on Avenida Europa (for details of all these places, *see page 79*).

If you can stick the pace and make it right through the night, then finish off by catching a taxi for an early morning cup of hot chocolate after 7.30am at **Chocolatería Valor**, Avenida del Paîs Valenciano 14

Left: Benidorm was a small fishing village only 50 years ago

The Centre
Alicante

8. ALICANTE CITY *(see map, p37)*

A full day exploring Alicante on foot: the castle, museum and old town in the morning; a beach in the afternoon; the small museum of 20th-century art in the early evening.

Alicante (Alacant) is by no means only a tourist centre. Where the beaches end, a Mediterranean city with a life of its own begins. Less culturally dynamic than Barcelona and less buzzy than Valencia it may be, but it has a good dose of their qualities and on a far more accessible scale. The best way to get your bearings is to take the clanking lift up from the Paseo de Gomez to the **Castillo de Santa Bàrbara** (summer 10am–8pm, winter 9am–7pm; park on the opposite side of the road).

Today, after centuries of refortifying and bombardment, the castle is more impressive from below than from inside, but it is worth the trip up to the top for the panoramic views. Immediately to the south lies the heart of the city, its broad Rambla neatly dissecting the scrambled old town from the more spacious 19th-century grid of streets and shady plazas. To the north, a great arc of hotel and apartment skyscrapers curves round from the industrial port and a marina to San Juan's white beach and the rocky Cabo de la Huertas.

City's Origins

The first Alicante grew up right in the middle of the tourist suburbs, close to Albufereta beach. The Greeks gave this Iberian settlement the name Akra Leuke ('white peak'), from which came the Roman name of Lucentum and the Arab or *valenciano* name of Alacant. The Carthaginians used it as a port, and the Carthaginian general Hannibal is said to have unloaded his war elephants here before embarking on the long journey towards Rome. You can visit the site, called **Tossal de Manises** (Albufereta; five minutes walk from the tram station; June–Sept Tues–Sun 9am–noon, 7–10pm; Oct–May 10am–2pm, 4–6pm).

Before visiting the site it is worth seeing the spectacular new **Museo Arqueologico de Alicante**, MARQ, (Antiguo Hospital Provincial San Juan de Dios, Pza Dr Gómez Ulla s/n; Tues–Sat 10am–7pm, Sun and holidays 10am–2pm) behind the castle. Here you can learn about the background to prehistoric, Roman, Muslim and

Left: Alicante has a good selection of beaches
Right: the historic castle overlooks the port

medieval Alicante with the help of atmospheric visual displays with evocative soundtracks and press-button screens, and you can buy a combined ticket to Lucentum.

The stroll back towards the old town, past the newly restored Modernist central market, will lead you to a variety of interesting small shops selling everything from *paella* pans to cut-price shoes sold direct from the factory. Carrying on, walk past the 19th-century theatre down the busy Rambla and across into **Calle San Isidro** to arrive at **San Nicolás** (daily, winter: 7.30am–12.30pm and 5.30–8pm; summer: 7.30am–noon and 6–8.30pm), the town's 17th-century modestly scaled cathedral. Inside, in the Gothic cloister, a fountain trickles among the ornamental orange trees.

A stone's throw beyond the cathedral is the 18th-century *ayuntamiento* housed in the old **Casa Consistorial** (Mon–Fri 9am–2pm). It has stunning reliefs both back and front by Juan Batista Borja, who also carved the cathedral door. The first step is used as sea level for all altitude measurements made in Spain. The plaza's finest moment comes every July, on the last night of the *hogueras*, the city's biggest fiesta, when the mayor lights a trapeze-like fuse which sputters over the heads of the crowd towards a vast wooden sculpture in the middle of the square. As it bursts into flame, the crowd erupts and the **Nit del Foc**, when nearly 100 such bonfires burn in sequence through the city, has officially begun. The fiesta even has its own museum, the **Museo de las Hogueras** (Rambla Méndez Núnez 27; open Tue–Sun am and pm).

Lunch Options

All around the arcaded plaza and dotted around the old town are bars and restaurants that offer a *menú del día* (menu of the day). **Nou Manolín** – which is close to the bullring, a 10-minute walk away – is a cut above the rest, and bullfight lovers can take in the new **Museo Taurino** (Place de Toros; Mon–Fri 10.30am–2.30pm, 5–8pm, Sat 10.30am–1.30pm), dedicated to the exploits of renowned local bull-fighters.

For a quick snack on the seafront there are plenty of different options. After lunch, **Playa del Postiguet** is a good spot for sunbathing out of season, but when the crowds thicken

Above: Santa María church
Right: a corner of the Barrio Santa Cruz

alicante & surrounds

you may prefer to take a taxi to **Cabo de las Huertas**, a rocky beach about 20 minutes away.

Returning to the old town, walk up the pedestrianised **Calle Mayor** – the city's main shopping street until the 19th century and still bustling – to wander through the **Barrio Santa Cruz**, originally the Muslim part of town and now the most atmospheric in a rakish way. Doves flutter around the gargoyle and cherub-laden façade of **Santa María** church, built over the main mosque. (The church opens for evening Mass at about 6pm.)

A short walk further back and up towards the castle you can see the **Pozos de Garrigós** (Plaza del Puente s/n), dating from the Islamic period. The four giant urn-like water cisterns were built underground to catch water as it poured down the mountain after heavy rainfall. They are currently closed for restoration. In Calle San Agustín, in a typical early 19th-century house, you can visit the **Museo de Belenes**, a collection of Nativity figures made by Spain's top Nativity craftsmen (Tues–Sat 10am–2pm, Apr–Sept 5–8pm, Oct–Mar 4–7.30pm).

International Modernism

Close by are the **Museo Alicantino de Arte Contemporaneo (MACA)**, currently closed while a new wing is being built, and the **Museo de Bellas Artes Gravina (MUBAG)** (Calle Gravina 13–15; open Tues–Sun 10am–2pm, 4–8pm and 9pm in summer), an enjoyable mixed bag of medieval to 20th-century art and decorative arts from the province's past; it also holds interesting temporary exhibitions.

Behind the museum and Sta María church, small whitewashed streets alive with gossip and children's street-games wind around under the base of the castle's mound. On the slopes above lies the **Parque de la Ereta**, a beautifully laid out park with children's water games, a restaurant and

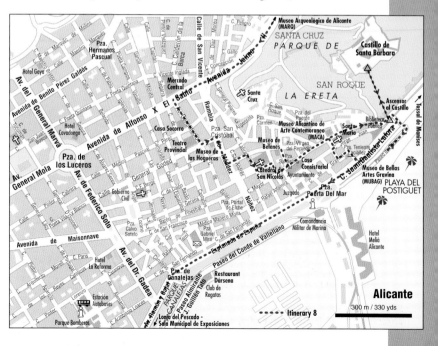

a solarium. Or you may like to join local families down by the sea on the
Explanada for the evening paseo. You
can stop off at **Peret's** legendary seafront
kiosk to grab a *horchata* (tiger-nut milk),
a refreshing drink in which the locals
like to dunk slabs of almond cake and
sponge fingers.

Afterwards, wander under the shade
of the huge ficus and palm trees, past the
municipal bandstand, to the modernist
fish market now restored as an exhibition centre. On the wharves at either end
of the harbour is the port's new leisure
complex. At **Darsena** you can sample 50
types of rice with fish and seafood while
looking over the harbour *(see page 75)*.

The nightlife in Alicante is never dull.
Depending on your tastes there is plenty
of action in the bars of the Barrio Santa Cruz and in the discos of San
Juan *(see page 78)*, which can be easily reached by tram.

9.CRAFT TRADITIONS:NOUGAT AND POTTERY IN JIJONA AND AGOST *(see map, p46–47)*

**From Alicante visit traditional diverse factories and workshops; you
should allow four hours for this itinerary.**

Many of Alicante's industries, including shoes, toys, textiles, paper, rugs,
ceramics and confectionery, have their roots in traditional crafts. Two of
the best examples are *turrón*-making in **Jijona** (Xixona) and the potteries
and industrial ceramics factories of **Agost**, which have preserved their artisan
roots and small-scale family ownership. Jijona, which is half an hour's drive
from Alicante on the road to Alcoi, is the home of Spanish *turrón*, a rich

honey-and-almond nougat, which comes either soft and sticky like an oily *halva*, hard and white like French Montelimar, or caramelised and glistening around whole almonds (known as Jijona, Alicante and *guirlache* respectively). Most of the 50 million kilos of *turrón* eaten in Spain every Christmas are made here, in small family factories that operate on a semi-artisanal basis, the almonds sorted by hand, the traditions passed down the generations. Job contracts are seasonal, for the winter only, and the workers usually move elsewhere for the summer, often running ice cream parlours.

One of the factories, **Turrones El Lobo** (Ctra de Busot km 1; Mon–Fri 10am–7.30pm, Sat 2–4pm, Sun 2–5pm; tel: 96 561 0225), organises half-hour visits round the work floor and its private museum, with old manual pestles and mortars, primitive curved-stone rolling boards and wood-fired crucibles turned by donkeys. The factory shop has every conceivable kind of *turrón* to take home – be realistic and bear in mind the state of your teeth when you make your choice.

Family Potteries

The road to Agost, which has been a pottery town since Roman times, winds up and down over the arid white Serra del Maigmó and past the **Tibi dam** *(see page 43)*. Artisan production here has adapted to the times: the town now survives due to its factories' new direction – the manufacture of industrial ceramics and roof tiles. But it still preserves half a dozen or so of the family potteries, which continue to manufacture the old-fashioned, unglazed *botijos*, or earthenware water bottles, that cool the water they contain by a process of evaporation. To work well, they have to be made from the right kind of clay (which is found around Agost) and wood-fired in a brick kiln.

Unfortunately, the traditional *botijos* are slowly losing their place to more modern industries. Some of the potters have survived by adapting to the world of today. **Emili Boix**, for example, repre-senting the eighth generation to work in the family pottery concern, tends to create mainly decorative ceramics – some painted in the classical Iberian style. Other potters, such as **The Molla Brothers**, Boix's neighbours, stick largely to the production of traditional functional pieces fired in a traditional kiln, which they will show you. Both potteries are easily found on the main road where it winds out of the top of the town.

A visit to the nearby **Museo de Alfarería** (Tues–Sun, summer: 11am–2pm, 5–8pm; winter: 11am–2pm; tel: 96 569 1199) is also worthwhile, and will undoubtedly further your appreciation of the pottery here and elsewhere in the region. The museum's excellent displays on the history of the potteries illustrate the different forms and techniques used. If the owner of the museum has time, she might well be persuaded to show you the chapel of **Santas Justa e Rufina**, patron saints of potters, in the **Calle de Alfarería** – the inside is decorated with wonderful small figures that were made at the time the chapel was built in the 1820s. From the chapel it is a short walk up to the honey-coloured old town, where you will find plenty of bars for snacks or a refreshing drink.

If you would like to extend the trip into a full day, you could stay and have lunch in Jijona, which is known especially for *giraboix* – a warming double dish of a broth thickened with egg yolks and a stew consisting of potatoes, white beans and salt-cod – and take in a visit to **Monóvar**'s arts and crafts museum *(see page 45)*.

10. VILLENA AND ELX *(see map, p46–47)*

A visit to the Iberian gold collection at Villena; in the afternoon a 45-minute drive to the Iberian–Roman site outside Elx, plus Europe's largest palm forest in the town centre.

At a first glance, **Villena** and **Elx** – or Elche – have little in common: Villena is a bustling small town in the Vinalopó valley, known for the striking silhouette of its medieval castle and for the strength of its wine; Elx is a dusty city, associated with its date palm forest, mystery plays and mushrooming shoe factories.

Under the surface though – quite literally – the two share buried treasures. In 1897 some farm workers inadvertently stumbled upon a stone

sculpture that has since become a symbol of the sophistication of Iberian culture. Unfortunately for Elx, the *Dama de Elche*, a serenely enigmatic figure, made her way via dealers to Paris and then back to Madrid, where she maintains pride of place in the Museo Arqueológico. (Central government has made it clear that she will not be returned to her place of origin but Elx continues to campaign for the statue's return). Since the initial discovery, however, a large number of other riches have turned up on the same Iberian and Roman site, where the river city of Illici once stood. These Elx managed to keep and display.

An Iberian Treasure Trove

A trip to **Villena** transports you even further back into the prehistoric past – another 50,000 or so years. Start the day here in the lovely 17th-century *ayuntamiento*, where the **Museo Arqueológico** (Pl. Santiago 1; Tues–Fri 10am–2pm, 5–8pm; holidays, weekends 11am–2pm; call ahead, tel 96 580 1150) is squeezed into one room. This extraordinary museum represents the life's work of one man, José María Soler, who died in 1996. The star attraction is an incredible Iberian treasure-trove that consists of 30 pieces of solid fluvial gold – bowls and small pots moulded and beaten to look like sea urchins, stunningly beautiful necklaces, bracelets weighing up to half a kilo (1 lb) each and giant earstuds. Soler found these priceless items in

Above: José María Soler with part of the treasure. **Above Right:** a street in Villena
Right: Villena is dominated by its medieval castle

the mid-1960s when he was working as a civil servant for the post office. Researchers believe the relatively advanced metal-working techniques, for example the methods of drilling, come from the Tartessan civilisation.

The rest of the collection, which frequently gets overlooked, comes from the large number of nearby ancient sites, one of them the Bronze Age capital of Cabeza Redonda – where the treasure was found – and another, called the Casa de Lara, which is unique in that it straddles 8,000 years of history and technological development. Other gems include a second (smaller) gold 'treasure', a unique clay crucible, a drinking bottle with a double mouth – perhaps for *anís* and water, and craftwork made from *esparto* grass and rush from a new site at Terlinques.

A Controversial Font

While in Villena, visit the 15th- and 16th-century church of **Santiago**, a fine example of Levantine Gothic architecture: its fluted cable columns, topped by lovely floral capitals, soar on up into high, shadowy vaulting, and next to the altar is a wonderful, richly carved font, also 16th-century, by sculptor Jacopo Florentino, one of Michelangelo's assistants, who settled in Villena. (The font spent many years in a backroom because the priest objected to the bared breasts on it.) Ask at the tobacconist opposite the side-door to visit the church during shop hours. You can also climb, past the rich baroque façade of the **Iglesia de Santa María** to the severe castle *(see page 49)*.

Elx

The quickest route to Elx is via the motorway to Alicante. It is then only a short drive to the **Parc Arqueològici Museu de L'Alcúdia** (Tues–Sat; Oct–Mar: 10am–5pm; Apr–Sept: 10am–2pm, 4–8pm, Sun 10am–2pm; small entrance fee), on the site of **Illici**, one of the country's most important Iberian sites. Be warned that it is badly signposted in town – follow signs to Dolores and watch for the turnoff at 2.2km). The museum is a labour of love, this time by the Ramos family, who own the farm and now boast three generations

of archaeologists. Astonishingly, given the value of the site, only one tenth of it has so far been excavated, although the family organises student digs every summer. The 3,000 pieces on show and the highlights of the site itself deserve at least an hour of the visitor's time.

Back in the centre, in the east wing of the **Alcázar** or **Palau de Altamira** (Tues–Sat 10am–1.30pm, 4.30–8pm; weekends, Sun and holidays 10.30am–1.30pm; entrance fee) is the town's answer to the Museo Arqueológico, where prize pieces from Alcudia are on show. Check out the pair of prowling sphinxes and a headless Roman Venus. The Palacio's walls and towers are also open. From here it is a short walk to the other monuments in the centre: the Muslim **Calaforra**, or watchtower, with its *mudéjar* hallway and, just beyond, the 16th-century façade of the **Convento de la Mercè.**

The Last Mystery Play

Behind the Convento are the well-restored **Banys Arabs** (Muslim baths; Tues–Sat 10am–1.30pm, 4.30–8pm, Sun 10.30am–1.30pm); the *ayuntament*, with its 14th-century clock striking on the quarter hour; and the overwhelming baroque **Basílica** (daily 7am–1.30pm, 5.30–9pm). The tower (open 11am–6pm; entrance fee) gives stunning views. Here, the spectacular **Misterio de Elx** takes place every August. The play tells of the Assumption of the Virgin Mary in a sung drama during which she is lowered from the dome by aerial machinery. It is the only European mystery play that has kept its medieval form (a 14th-century text) and is still performed by townspeople in a church designed around the play. Book tickets well in advance from the Elx tourist office or see the virtual show at the Museu de la Festa close to the castle. The final *Nit de l'Alba* features a stunning, explosive fireworks display.

The glorious small monastery church of **San José**, a 15-minute walk away on the far side of the river, is well worth the effort for its refreshingly humble Franciscan version of baroque, with original frescoes, *azulejos* and woodcarving. You can stroll there and back over La Pasarela and through the former Muslim quarter, or Raval, marked out by its tightly packed streets. Have a drink at La Glorieta before visiting the **Hort del Cura** (Tues–Sun

Above: Elx locals take their leisure seriously

9am–7.30pm, closes at 8.30pm in summer; entrance fee), the botanical garden in the palm forest. The palm forests have now been added to the UNESCO cultural heritage list. The Hort, laid out in the 19th century, is best known for the Imperial Palm, a hermaphrodite palm tree that changed sex after about 70 years of life and sprouted seven new trunks, one of which produces dates. But for many it is the artfulness of the planting between the palms, the contrasts between cactuses and lilies, that makes the garden so seductive.

Tailoring supper to the size of your pocket, you can choose between various restaurants *(see page 76)*, where you can try the great local speciality of *arroz con costra*, rice with pork and sausages buried under a golden egg crust.

11. A PICNIC AT TIBI RESERVOIR *(see map, p46–47)*

An excursion to see one of the oldest working reservoirs and dams in Europe, located a 50-minute drive inland from Alicante.

It might seem that the village of **Tibi** has little to make it stand out from countless other villages in the inland sierras of Alicante: it has a few shops and bars, a village cooperative and a shady main street. What makes it worth visiting, however, are its working reservoir and dam, built over 14 years at the end of the 16th century (1580–94) to irrigate the Alicante *huerta*.

The reservoir and dam are most easily reached off the A-36 **autoría** from Alicante. Shortly after km 16, turn right for a garage 200 metres (660ft) before the turn-off to **Agost** (if you get lost, ask at the garage for the *pantano*). From here the reservoir is signposted; you will come to

Above: Elx's baroque Basílica
Right: the Tibi dam

a gate at the end of the road. Leave the car here and walk the final kilometre. There is a choice of two approaches to the dam, one a short cut up the slope to your left, which brings you straight out on top of the dam; the alternative option is more spectacular for those with a head for heights. This route heads down a path to the right to a small bridge with a plaque dedicated to Charles IV, from where you get the first complete view of the dam, directly upstream.

Built between a narrow gorge, the dam's overall dimensions are nothing like those of many modern dams, but the severe curved wall, making brilliant use of the natural geography, is a magnificent sight when you stand below it, listening to the eerie sound effects of the water and air eddying within. Watch the overflow splash from above, down onto the rocks below.

A dizzying climb of more than 100 steps cut into the rock, with only a crumbling rail to hold, takes you up to the top of the dam. Set into its worn blocks of stone is a plaque commemorating its refurbishment in 1794. This is a wonderful place to have a picnic, looking out onto the reservoir on one side and down the wall of the dam on the other. Returning to Alicante on the autoría it is a short diversion to Agost *(see page 38)*.

12. THE WINE COUNTRY OF MONOVAR
(see map, p46–47)

Monóvar is about a 45-minute drive from Alicante. Allow two hours to visit the town, and another three hours to explore the surrounding wine villages.

Until the end of the 19th century, Monóvar's red wine was among the most sought-after in Europe. Transparent and slightly sweet, it was said to be an aphrodisiac, probably on account of its high alcohol content. It was also among the most expensive: in the late 19th century, during a golden age that Monóvar enjoyed following the destruction of French vineyards by phylloxera, a single shipload covered the entire building costs of the casino in Monóvar three times over. Tastes in wine changed however, and the French vineyards were replanted. Today the vineyards of Monóvar are little known although its dessert wines are considered among the best in Spain

by native connoisseurs. In summer the *bodegas* are usually open from 9am until 2pm; the rest of the year you can also taste and buy later in the afternoon (4–7pm). From the coast, take the back road from Alicante via **Agost** *(see page 38)* and **Novelda** *(see page 48)*. You pass first through almond groves and then into the vineyards. Trellised vines run in an unbroken sea until they rise, banked in hillside terraces, to meet the sierras looming in the background. The native Monastrel grapes are largely used for making red wine; Verdil for white.

A Leaning Clock Tower

Monóvar (Monóver) is only a small town, but it has an interesting character. The clock tower leans drunkenly at the top of the town, and the church is missing one of its bell towers. A 19th-century pharmacy and shop are on display at the **Museo de Artes y Oficios** (Calle Salamanca 6; Mon–Fri 10am–2pm, 4–6pm, Sat 11am–2pm, by advance arrangement; tel: 96 547 0270). For Spaniards, Monóvar is famous for being the birthplace of **Azorín,** a prolific essayist, novelist and politician of the late 19th century.

Among the *bodegas*, **Salvador Poveda** (Calle Benjamín Palencia; daily 7am–3pm), the biggest, is right in the centre of town. Salvador Poveda is famous for its fragrant pudding wine, Fondillón, which is apparently King Juan Carlos's favourite after-dinner tipple. Fondillón needs to be matured for 20 years (beware of cheap imitations), but the *bodega* also produces blood-coloured reds and excellent, delicate rosés. Their character comes from the local wine-making method, in which the rosé is fermented from must drawn off during a first light crushing of the grapes; the red is derived from a *doble pasta* in which the first batch of must and grapes is mixed with a second one prior to fermentation. Another family *bodega* on the edge of town, **Primitivo Quiles**, produces similar wines and delicious vermouth.

From Monóvar, you can continue on a short circular route which takes you around the **Sierra de Reclot** and through a number of other wine villages – **Hondón** (where a cooper still works), **Mañar**, **Culebrón**, **Pinoso**, **Algueña** and **La Romana**. The landscape here will change dramatically when a major new reservoir is built in the coming years. These villages are known for their earthy country cuisine, especially rice with rabbit and snails, and *gazpachos*, which here is a type of game stew *(see page 73)*. Go easy on the wine, though, especially if you have been tasting – at Culebrón, they say it is strong enough to revive dead men.

Left: the fruit of the fields
Above: refreshments in a local bar

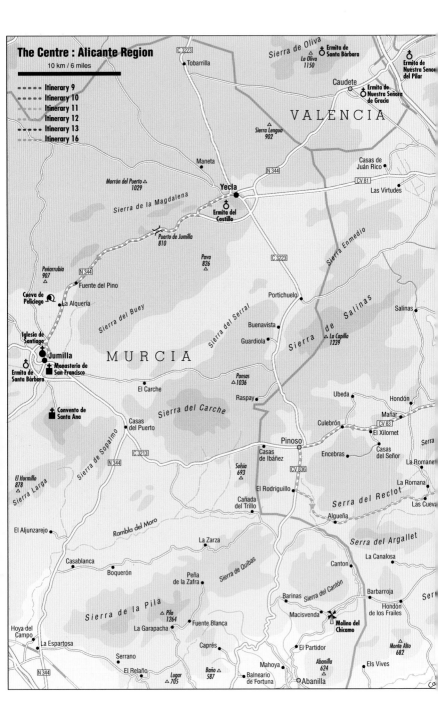

The Centre : Alicante Region

10 km / 6 miles

----- Itinerary 9
----- Itinerary 10
----- Itinerary 11
----- Itinerary 12
----- Itinerary 13
----- Itinerary 16

C 3223
Tobarrilla

Sierra de Oliva
La Oliva 1150
Ermita de Santa Bárbara
Ermita de Nuestra Senora del Pilar

Caudete
Ermita de Nuestra Señora de Gracia

V A L E N C I A

Sierra Lengua 902

Maneta

Casas de Juan Rico

N 344
Yecla
CV 81
Las Virtudes

Morrón del Puerto 1029

Sierra de la Magdalena

Ermita del Castillo

Puerto de Jumilla 810

Pava 826

C 3223

Sierra Enmedío

Peñarrubia 907
N 344
Fuente del Pino

Cueva de Peliciego
La Alquería

Portichuelo

Sierra de Salinas
Salinas

Sierra del Buey

Sierra del Serral

Buenavista
Guardiola

La Capilla 1239

Iglesia de Santiago

Jumilla
Monasterio de San Francisco

M U R C I A

Ermita de Santa Bárbara

El Carche

Pansas 1036

Raspay

Ubeda
Hondón

Mañar
CV 83

Convento de Santa Ana

Casas del Puerto

Sierra del Carche

Culebrón
El Xilornet

Pinoso
Encebras
Casas del Señor
Serra
La Romane

Sierra de Sopalmo

C 3213
N 344

Casas de Ibáñez

CV 836

El Hormillo 878
Sierra Larga

Solsia 693

El Rodriguillo

La Romana
Las Cueva

Serra del Reclot

El Aljunzarejo

Rambla del Moro

Cañada del Trillo

Algueña

La Zarza

Serra del Argallet

Casablanca

Boquerón

Peña de la Zafra

Sierra de Quibas

La Canalosa
Canton

Barbarroja
Ser

Sierra de la Pila

Pila 1264
La Garapacha
Fuente Blanca

Barinas
Sierra del Cantón

Macisvenda

Molino del Chicamo

Hondón de los Fraíles

Hoya del Campo
La Espartosa

Caprés

El Partidor

Monte Alto 682

Serrano

El Relaño

Lugar 705
Baño 587

Mahoya
Balneario de Fortuna

Abanilla 624

Abanilla

Els Vives

N 344

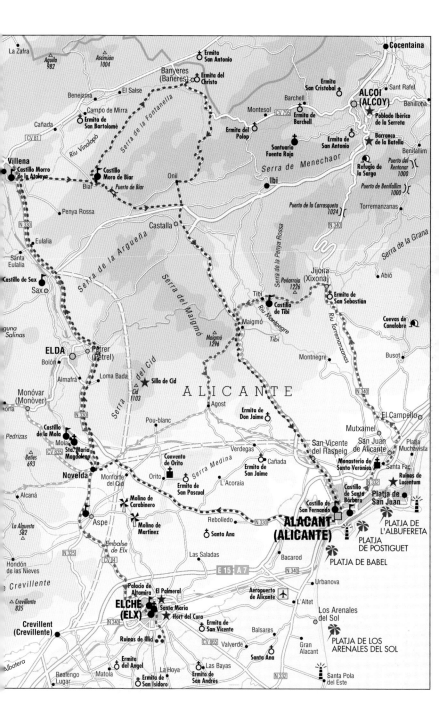

13. FRONTIER TERRITORY: THE VINALOPO VALLEY
(see map, p46–47)

Starting at Alicante, you can spend a day visiting a series of castles in the Vinalopó valley. For a half-day itinerary, turn back at Biar (Bihar).

The broad valley floor of the **Vinalopó** has always been both a strategic route and frontier territory. This is where the cultures of the Bronze Age separated into different forms, where the Carthaginians were defeated by the Romans, and where the Muslim kingdom of Murcia met its northern boundary. Later Castile battled with Aragon here for more than a century. Today, perched on rocky outcrops, medieval castles stand as silent markers of the old Muslim and Christian frontiers. The fortresses preside over almond trees, olive groves and vineyards where table grapes ripen inside paper bags during the autumn.

Now that the castles have no military function, it is easy to forget their former importance. As Philip V wrote in 1704, during the War of Spanish Succession, 'It is more important for me to keep Alicante than Valencia, because if Valencia were lost, which God forfend, it alone will be lost; but if Alicante were lost, both Valencia and Castile would be lost.'

An Impregnable Tower

The castle of **Santa Bárbara** in Alicante, which was a virtually impregnable tower in Muslim times, features many later additions (*see page 35* for visiting times). Among its surviving elements, the most fascinating are the 16th- and 17th-century additions (modelled on the French Vauban system) and the sheer scale of the walled area, which could garrison up to 40,000 men.

From Alicante, follow signs to Madrid along the motorway to reach **Novelda** (about 40 minutes drive). Just beyond is the castle of **La Mola**, which is famous for its superb 12th-century triangular tower, designed by Ibrahim

Above: Sax's Hispano-Arabic castle

of Tunis, a famous Arab military engineer. The tower stands above an eye-catching small modernist sanctuary designed by Sala, a disciple of the inimitable Antonio Gaudí. Back in the town you might also want to visit the perfectly preserved **Casa Museo Modernista** (Calle Mayor 22–4; Mon–Thur 9am–2pm, 4–7pm, Fri 9am–2pm, 4–6pm). It is then a 15-minute drive up the motorway to **Villena**. The journey passes two more Hispano-Arabic castles: **Petrel** and **Sax**. The latter has an extraordinary setting – it is perched like an eagle's nest above the old town (the key is kept in the *ayuntamiento*). Both castles have been much restored.

For this reason, Villena's castle, **La Atalaya** (literally, 'the watchtower'), is more impressive when seen from close up. Heavily fortified by the Almohades in the 12th century – their brick vaulting survives inside the superb keep – it became the centre of a powerful feudal state owing allegiance to Castile. The castle controlled, and was in turn protected by, a string of smaller castles: **La Mola**, **Sax**, **Elda** and, in Albacete province on the road to Madrid, **Chinchilla** and **Almansa**. In the 15th century it fell into the hands of the Pachecos, the hugely powerful masters of the Order of Santiago. They built the thick double outer walls and furnished it as an aristocratic home. You can walk right around the walls; the splendid keep and tower are due to reopen for guided visits in 2004 after restoration.

Castle Towns

From Villena, you can take either of two routes. The shorter of these takes the road to **Biar** on the Aragonese side of the old border. The prettiest of all these castle towns, Biar has a hilly old quarter that rises sharply as you climb up the long flights of steps to reach the castle. It was the scene of a hard-fought battle in the Reconquest and it features the oldest surviving example of octagonal Almohad vaulting. Outside the town are a snow-well, ceramicist and several country restaurants.

The longer option loops north to the town of **Bañeres** (Bañyeres de la

Mariola), which has a Gothic church and yet another Hispano-Arabic castle (the key is at Calle Castillo 20; ring in advance to arrange to pick it up; tel: 96 656 7315 or 96 656 7756). This castle was in Aragonese hands after the Reconquest. It looks out over four provinces – Valencia, Murcia, Albacete and Alicante – and marks part of the border between *castellano-* and *valenciano-* speaking territories.

The town's attractions include a small paper-making museum (Museu Molí Paperer) and access to the new Sierra de Mariola Natural Park.

Left: a public fountain in Biar

14. SOUTHERN COSTA BLANCA: ALICANTE TO DEHESA

(see map, p52–53)

The coast road south from Alicante passes Santa Pola, where you can take a boat to Tabarca island. Further south, past pine forests, Guardamar is 1¼ hours drive from Alicante.

The road south from Alicante cuts through a flat, luminous landscape past an open shoreline. Only dusty palms, apartment blocks and housing estates seem to break the long stretches of sand. Closer inspection, however, reveals the fortified island and aquarium at the lively fishing port of Santa Pola; a string of salt pans which are now protected as nature reserves; and some fine unspoilt beaches.

Santa Pola is the most interesting of the southern resorts once you have made it to the seafront (parking available). The most attractive road from the north, reached through the Gran Alacant estate, runs along Calabassí beach. Next to the port, home to the largest deep sea and coastal fleet of the Mediterranean, you can catch a boat to **Tabarca** *(for sailings see page 93)*, the main island of a small archipelago in the bay, which Charles III fortified and settled with Genoese prisoners in the 18th century. The walled

town now looks like a grandiose folly, the unfinished church and entrance arch absurdly oversized next to the squat fishermen's cottages. On the other half of the island is the old lighthouse and solar station that generates the island's electricity. (A walk around the island takes about 1½ hours.)

A Double Life

The island now has only about 100 residents. In winter they work on the fishing boats and in summer they work in the excellent fish restaurants. There is very good snorkelling and sub-aqua diving in the protected waters around the island. Ecologists consider the marine reserve that surrounds the archipelago a model of its type; it has helped to regenerate fishing stocks by protecting breeding grounds.

You can stay on the island until sunset, when it is at its emptiest and most beautiful. Back in Santa Pola it is worth catching the aquarium and clinic for sick turtles in the **Plaza Francisco Fernández Ordoñez** (Tues–Sun, summer: 11am–1pm, 6–10pm; winter: 10am–1pm, 5–7pm; entrance fee) and the Museo de la Pesca, a fishing museum in the city-centre castle (open all week 11am–1pm, 4–7pm; entrance fee). Afterwards you might head for one of the busy fish restaurants *(see page 77)*. The most interesting local dish is *gazpachos de pescado*, a marine adaptation of the inland game stews, but all the usual rices and *caldero* are excellent too.

If you decide to continue going south, the beach road south from the town centre brings you out abruptly at huge white mounds of salt extracted from

Above: return of the fishermen. **Above Right:** on Tabarca island
Right: the Santa Pola–Tabarca ferry

the chequered salt-pans, a natural park since 1994. The park was formed to protect the flamingos, grebes and other migratory birds – some 250 recorded species – that pass through here every spring and autumn. A 20-minute drive south will take you to the beach of La Marina, backed by pine glades planted on the dunes that run south all the way to **Guardamar de Segura**. The beach is now being overtaken by high-rise tourist blocks, but the pine groves around the mouth of the River Segura have become a park, in the middle of which you can visit a mosque unearthed from a thick blanket of sand. In the town itself are a number of fish restaurants specializing in the local *langostines* and *caldero*.

Further south, behind the massive concrete sprawl of **Torrevieja** – one of Spain's fastest-growing resorts made up largely of holiday flats and homes – two larger salt lakes cover a total of 2,100 hectares (5,200 acres). They still produce a million tons of salt a year, but are now also a bird reserve with walking tours starting from the information centre (Tues–Sun 9am–2.30pm, Oct–Mar also 4–6pm). In the town itself, there is a small **Museo del Mar y la Sal** (C. Patricio Perez 10; Mon–Sun 9am–2pm, 5.30–9pm, weekends closes 1.30pm). Another part of the harbour is used to stage the summer song festival dedicated to the Latin American *habaneras* that were brought back here in the 19th century by emigrants *(see p 85)*. Just down the road, on the Paseo Vista Alegre, is the splendid *fin de siècle* **Casino** where you can sit and watch the locals go about their business over a drink and a snack. For more deserted beaches and a refreshing afternoon swim, drive on to the far end of **Dehesa de Campoamor**, avoiding the splurges of building. Here rust-coloured cliffs drop down to small coves, and the water is warm enough for swimming well into the autumn.

alicante & surrounds

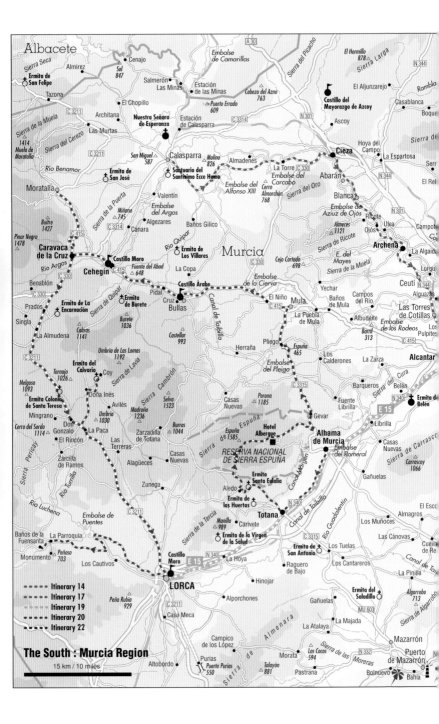

Albacete

Murcia

The South : Murcia Region

15 km / 10 miles

- - - - Itinerary 14
- - - - Itinerary 17
- - - - Itinerary 19
- - - - Itinerary 20
- - - - Itinerary 22

Solsia 693
Encebrás
La Romaneta
Monforte del Cid
Ermita de San Pascual
Cañada

CV 836
El Rodriguillo
La Romana
Novelda
Orito
L'Acoraia

ALACANT (ALICANTE)

Cañada del Trillo
Serra del Reclot
Las Cuevas
Alcaná
Molino de Carabinero
Rebolledo

IN 330
Santa Ana
Bacarod

La Zarza
Algueña
Sierra del Argallet
La Alguesta 582
Aspe
Molino de Martínez
Las Saladas

IN 340
Urbanova

Peña de la Zafra
Barinas
Barbarroja
La Canalosa
Hondón de las Nieves

CV 84
Aeropuerto de Alicante
E 15 A 7

Los Arenales del Sol

Pila 1264
Fuente Blanca
Macisvenda
Molina del Chicamo
Hondón de los Frailes
Crevillente
Crevillent (Crevillente)

ELCHE (ELX)
Balsares

CV 865
Valverde
Gran Alacant

La Garapacha
Caprés
Mahoya
El Partidor
Monte Alto 682
Alicante
IN 340
Matola
Ermita del Angel
La Hoya
Las Bayas
Santa Ana

IN 332
Santa Pola del Este

Baño 587
Abanilla
Els Vives
Canal de Albatera
Realengo
Lugar
Casa de Lleo
Ermita de San Anton
Platja Lissa
Santa Pola

Lugar 705
Balneario de Fortuna
Los Vicentes
Albatera
A 37
Sant Isidre d'Albatera
Catral

Salinas del Bras del Port
PLATJA DEL PINET

Fenazar
Fortuna
La Matanza
Ermita de Sta. Filomena
Benferri
Granja de Rocamora
Cox
Dolores
La Marina del Pinel
Pinet
Golfo de Santa Pola
PLATJA DE LA MARINA

C 3223
Izquierda
Margen
Embalse de Santomera
E 15 A 7
Callosa de Segura
El Saladar
Almoradí
San Fulgencio
PLATJA DE LA PINADA

Ermita de la Hornera
Ermita de Beltrán
ORIHUELA (ORIOLA)
La Aparecida
Rafal
CV 914
Formentera del Segura
CV 920
Guardamar del Segura
PLATJA DE GUARDAMAR

Molina de Segura
Santomera
Siscar
Río Segura
CV 95
Bigastro
Benejúzar
Rojales
Benijófar
Dunas de Guardamar

Cabezo de Torres
Los Pavos
Beniel
Desamparados
Hurchillo
Jacarilla
Castillo de Montemar
Salines de la Mata

IN 301
bera
Molina
Las Lumbreras
Alquerías
Zeneta
Serra del Cristo
El Mojón
Los Montesinos
CV 905
NUEVA PLATJA

San Jerónimo
Monteagudo
Embassament de la Pedrera
La Mata

MURCIA
Torreagüera
Cabezo de la Plata
Torremendo
Salines de Torrevieja
Torre del Moro

La Nora
IN 340
Beniaján
Torremendo
San Miguel de Salinas
Lomas Altas

Palmar
IN 301
Algezares
Columbares 647
Rebate
Los Balcones
La Veleta
Torrevieja

ngonera Verde
Santuario de la Fuensanta
Puerto de San Pedro 320
Sierra de Escalona
Las Filipinas
Villamartín
Punta Prima

Puerto de la Cadena 340
Castillo de la Luz
Sucina
El Pinar
Castillo de D. Juan
La Zenia
PLATJA FLAMENCA

Parador del Carmen
Aviteses
Dehesa de Campoamor
Cap Roig
PLATJAS DE ORIHUELA

Baños y Mendigo
Molino
Pilar de la Horadada
Torre de la Horadada

Corvera
Murta
Los Martínez
Balsicas
San Cayetano
Pozo Aledo
Lo Pagán
El Mojón
Cotorillo
PLAYA DEL MOJÓN

IN 301
Roldán
Lo Ferro
San Javier
Santiago de la Ribera
Punta de Algas

Valladolises
Balsa Pintada
Gimenado
Dolores
Roda
San Javier
Punta del Pudrider
PLAYA DEL PUDRIMAL

El Estrecho
Lobosillo
Santa Rosalía
PLAYA DE PALO
Faro del Estacio
PLAYA DEL ESTACIO

Fuente Álamo
Aibujón
Las Lomas
Torre Pacheco
Los Alcázares
Mar Menor
I. Perdiguera
PLAYA DEL PEDRUCHO

El Pericón 372
El Aljorra
Pozo Estrecho
La Puebla
El Carmolí
I. Mayor
PLAYA DE MARCHAMALO

Torre de la Campana
Miranda
Santa Ana
La Palma
El Carmolí
Los Urrutias
PLAYA DE LOS NIETOS

Cuesta Blanca
Llagostera
La Aparecida
IN 332
El Algar
Los Nietos
La Manga del Mar Menor
Islas Hormigas

Los Ruices
Perín
Tallante
Martagones
Los Dolores
La Unión
MU 312
Playa Honda
Cabo de Palos

Minas de Colóm
CARTAGENA
Castillo de la Atalaya
Catedral
C 345
Llano del Beal
Los Belones
Atamaria
Cabo de Palos

Portús
IN 332
Castillo de San Julián
Alumbres
Portman
Área de Minas
PLAYA DE CALBLANQUE

Plana
La Azohía
Castillo de las Galera
Escombreras
PLAYA DEL GORGUEL
PLAYAS LARGA & PARREÑO

c o s t a   c a l i d a

The South
Murcia Region

15. MURCIA CITY: SPANISH BAROQUE *(see map, p56)*
A full day exploring Murcia's unique baroque art and architecture.

Murcia is a wonderfully satisfying tourist city: there's so much to see, and yet all of it is within easy walking distance. In summer the breezeless heat is intense, beating you back off the streets for long rests in cafés or ice-cream-parlours. Ideally, you need to come in spring or autumn and allow several days, so that you can wander at leisure around the shops, parks and museums, and, in the mellow evenings, get under the skin of the southern street life. The busiest time is Holy Week, when you can see the processions and the explosively colourful spring fiestas which follow close on its heels.

If you have only one day, then concentrate on the city's hoard of baroque art and architecture. It is splendid, it is unique and, even for those who think they don't like baroque, it is fascinating because it captures the spirit of the place. Here, distilled in stone and marble and painted wood, are the exuberance of the fertile *huerta*, the drama of religious fervour, and the love of ornamental detail inherited from the Muslim centuries.

They are all shown in detail in the **Museo de la Ciudad** (Pl. Agustinas 5; Tues–Sat 10am–2pm, 5–8pm, Sun 11am–2pm; weekdays only in summer), which tells the city's story in a lively way with sounds and interactive displays on everything from prehistoric food and Muslim art to the famous Nativity figures made by local potters today.

The **Cathedral** (open daily 7am–1pm, 5–8pm) is best approached through the **Plaza Cardinal Belluga** so that your first impression is of the superb main façade. Designed by Valencian architect and sculptor Jaime Bort, it is a perfect balance of ornament and structure, a symbolic gateway to the region, brilliantly adapted to the building and its setting. Other highlights of the Cathedral, which was originally the site of the Great Mosque, are the **Capilla de los Vélez**, its 15th-century white stone stun-ningly embroidered with detail inside (it is regarded as one of the best examples of Isabelline Gothic architecture) and the cathedral **museum** (10am–1pm, 5–7pm, 8pm in summer).

From here, take a quick look at the crumbling **bishop's palace** and the lovely oval **Iglesia de San Juan de Dios** (Tues–Sat 10am–2pm; Oct–Mar 5–8.30pm and Sun am) restored in 1996, then cross the river to the **Plaza de Camachos** (intended to be oval), where the city's bullfights were held. Both this and the **Puente Viejo**, with its curious shrine at one end, were worked on by Bort as part of the remodelling of the city centre. The motifs of his work – the

Left: Murcia cathedral
Right: stained glass at the 19th-century Casino, Murcia

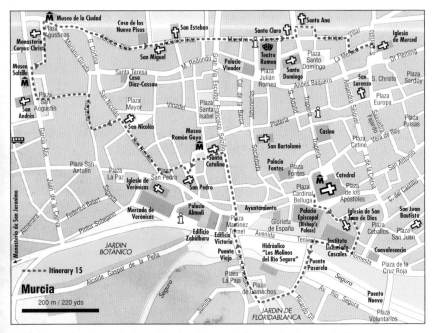

broken arched cornice, the allegorical figures, the decorated columns – are echoed in buildings elsewhere in the city.

Baroque Masterclass

The essence of Murcian baroque can be seen in the work of Francisco Salzillo (1707–83), the sculptor whose life-size processional figures and altarpieces adorn so many of the churches around the region. The realism Salzillo added to these idealised figures, capturing them in mid gesture as if with the camera shutter, gives them a heightened dramatic quality and extraordinary emotional power. In part that skill was inherited from his father, a Neapolitan sculptor. The **Museo Salzillo** (Pl. San Augustín 3; Tues–Sat 10am–2pm, 5–8pm, Sun 11am–2pm; July and Aug weekdays only) exhibits nine massive *pasos*, processional groups that he carved between 1752 and 1778, and a collection of his nativity figures which reflect the same narrative qualities together with a closely observed realism.

On the way to the museum through the old town, you pass three churches – **San Pedro**, **Santa Catalina**, **San Nicolás** – and just beyond are another trio – **San Miguel**, **Santa Ana** and **Santa Clara** – all with fine façades and more Salzillos. Most are open for evening Mass every day, on Saturday afternoons and all day on Sundays. The **Iglesia de Merced** is also outstanding. There are plenty of bars and cafés en route for coffee and *aperitivos*.

Back in town, the baroque spirit was reincarnated in modernist form at the end of the 19th century. Among the examples scattered around the city, the **Casino** (9.30am–9.30pm; entrance fee), on Calle Trapería , decorated in the 1890s, is unmissable, with its wildly extravagant Arab and Pompeiian patios and plush 'ladies' cloakroom'. The **Casa de Andrés Almansa** also has an interesting modernist façade. They are both in the main shopping and bar area, which is a hive of activity in early evening.

A final interesting visit is the **Museo Ramón Gaya** (Pl. Santa Catalina; Tues–Sat 10am–2pm, 5–8pm, Sun 11am–2pm; weekdays only in summer) dedicated to the painter who, like so many of his generation, spent most of his life in political exile.

16. THE MURCIAN WINE COUNTRY: JUMILLA, YECLA AND BULLAS *(see map, p46–47)*

Allow 1 hour to reach Yecla from Alicante or 1¼ from Murcia city and 20 minutes on to Jumilla, for lunch in the market restaurant. Bullas' hilly vineyards lie 45 minutes drive west of Murcia city.

Where **Murcia** bulges north towards **La Mancha** and opens up into gentle sierras and plateaux, the horizons are wide and full of light, and the sparsely populated plains are cut across by straight roads; the farming land is planted with wheat, olives and vines. Of the three, it is the vines which dominate today. **Yecla** is the largest of the region's three up-and-coming wine denominations of origin (DOs). 'This good town of countrymen...' wrote the novelist Azorín in the early 20th century, 'they love, but love the earth...and they have enormous faith, the faith of the early mystics...this is the old Spain, legendary, heroic.'

The legacy of the faith is a string of churches. Cutting up towards the old town along Calle Perales and San Francisco, you will pass three of them along the way: **San Roque** (with a wonderful *mudéjar* wooden ceiling), **San Francisco** (Renaissance to baroque) and, further up, the massive blue-domed **Iglesia de la Purísima**, which the town struggled and scraped to build for a whole century (*c*1750–1868). At the very top, on the **Plaza Mayor**, stand the mellow-stoned Renaissance **granary** and 19th-century **corn exchange**, and the Church of **San Salvador**, badly damaged but with its 16th-century pyramidal tower intact. Note the carved frieze of faces under the parapet.

The agricultural base of the town has now disappeared, and is replaced

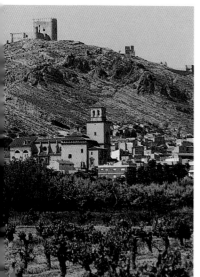

by furniture manufacturing which grew out of coopering. But the native Monastrell vines remain all-important. On the edge of town, at the massive **Cooperativa de la Purísima**, one of the largest in Spain, you can taste and buy the local reds, which vary between powerful table wines in the old style, with a lot of body and colour – sometimes called 'macho wines' – and smoother, fruity blends adapted to modern drinking tastes, for which the harvest is brought forward to reduce the sugar content of the grapes.

The reds from neighbouring

Left: a view of Jumilla

Jumilla, a 20-minute drive from Yecla, have been famed since Roman times. They are even more full-bodied (some are 16° strong), a result of intense summer heat and the age of the vines, which, unusually, were not damaged by phylloxera. On the way into town, at **La Alquería**, you will pass the co-operative of **San Isidro**, the town's largest *bodega*, which sells table wine from

the barrel, bottled vintages matured in oak (1973, 1980 and 1981 are prime years), *vino rancio* matured in wood, sweet *mistela* and delicious local cheeses resembling mild young Manchegos *(see page 72)*. For those who are interested, Jumilla also has a small wine museum (C. Garcia Lorca 1; tel: 679 788 251 to arrange visits).

Quite apart from the fame of its wines, Jumilla is a charming small market town. It boasts the 16th-century monastery of **Santa Ana** (with an eccentric museum of curiosities brought by Franciscans from all over the world), a private house designed by Gaudí, and **Casa Sebastián** – a wonderful market restaurant with crates of provisions stacked around the walls, hatches opening into the small kitchen and no written menu. Eat, drink from the ample cellar and enjoy *(see page 76)*. In August, crowds flock in for the wine fiesta, when a fountain flows with *vino tinto*.

Further south, in the hills west of Murcia city, is **Bullas**, the smallest of the region's denominations. It promises much: in 2000, one of its red wines won a major European prize. Here a small specialist company will organise tastings and trips to the vineyards or *bodegas* (Mundo Enológico; tel: 968 654 205).

17. DOWN THE SEGURA VALLEY: CALASPARRA TO MURCIA CITY *(see map, p52–53)*

The drive down the dramatically beautiful Segura Valley to Murcia city can be completed in 2 hours but is more enjoyable taken slowly over the course of the day: you can also continue through the flatter lower valley past historic Orihuela to an unusual Mediterranean garden at Jacarilla.

Following rivers is one of the best ways of exploring Spain. The **Segura** is no exception. Rising high in the sierras of Jaen, it slows to a glassy snake by the time it reaches Murcia city. But behind that deceptive quietness it is an immensely powerful river, irrigating a lush swathe of fruit orchards and citrus groves that cut through the dry sierras and plains, villages and towns, narrowing and widening around the river as it runs down to the coastal plain.

Join the river at **Calasparra**, famous for its rice fields ever since the time of Philip V. At this

Above: sampling the local wine
Left: citrus groves at Ojós

point it rushes through the spectacular **Cañón de los Almudenes**, which is signposted off the road along the left bank to Cieza. There is a place to swim here, but be careful: below the dam the water is extremely dangerous.

For the drive down to **Cieza**, double back to Calasparra and take the picturesque road along the right bank, passing a reservoir and pine forests before dropping down to the river and the lush *huerta* for the first time. Just before Cieza is the impressive Atalaya, with panoramic views, where the Muslim citadel of Sisáya was built into the rock. In the town centre the new **Museo de Siyasa** (Tues–Sat 9am–1.30pm, 2pm May–Sept and 5.30–9pm, Sun 10.30am–2pm) showcases the finds from this unique site, and organises limited access to the small, remarkably complete town.

A Land of Plenty

Follow the signs out of town for Blanca and Abarán. Here the valley suddenly narrows into the dramatically beautiful valley of **Ricote**, the road dipping and curving past plum and peach orchards, with the silhouette of Cieza castle perched above. These orchards are largely new, planted since the small dam at Ojós allowed irrigation some 12 years ago. But the citrus groves further down, at **Blanca** and **Ojós**, standing out against the mountainsides like an oasis in the desert, recreate a sense of Muslim Spain. This is not poetic licence: the Muslims first started irrigating the area in the 8th century, and they stayed here until 1611. Their imprint is all around you in the walled paths running between the groves and in the occasional water wheels at the side of the river. Many of these have now been replaced by electric pumps, but one of the largest working wheels in Europe, over 11 metres (36 feet) in diameter, is still in operation at Alberán as are another half dozen wheels along the river. A boat or canoe trip in this part of the valley can be organised from Blanca (tel: 968 778 124).

The **Vega Alta** – or upper river plain – ends in style at **Archena**, where 19th-century hotels stand over the thermal baths just outside town. Both the swimming pool in the sub-tropical gardens – you pay at the office – and the bar give a wonderful taste of *belle époque* elegance.

The road runs from here towards the small group of villages in the original Murcian *huerta*, or market garden, planted by the Romans and extended by the Arabs. Since the middle of the 19th century it has steadily expanded,

Above: water wheel at La Ñora

and now produces more lemons than any other region in Europe – as well as oranges, peppers, garlic and three crops a year of other vegetables and fruit. Inevitably, modern agribusiness now calls the tune here although the chimneys of the 19-century preserving factories still rise over **Molina de Segura**. The river itself has coped with the spread of intensive farming, but at the cost of pollution and drastically falling water levels.

Nonetheless, there are interesting reminders of past times: at **Javalí Nuevo**, the small 10th-century *contraparada*, which still stands in the river, and, at **Alcantarilla**, another *noria* or Arab water wheel, which has a double system of 'live' and 'dead' water, taking it from the river and putting

it back in again. It stands in the garden of the **Museo Etnológico de la Huerta** (Ctra de la Alcantarilla, by Alcantarilla turning; look for the water wheel on your right; Tues–Fri 10am–8pm, 10am–6.30pm in winter; weekends 10am– 1.30pm, 4–6pm; 10am–1pm and 3–6pm in winter). The displays of tools, costumes, ceramics, woodcarving and the reconstructed *barraca*, or cane and adobe cottage, describe a way of life that has now largely disappeared. All that remains today are a few words of the local dialect, *panocho*, the dances and songs of the spring fiestas, and the cuisine and the crafts that have now found a new lease of life.

It is a short drive from here into **Murcia city**, originally built in the 9th century as an ideal place to bridge the river. After crossing over the **Puente Viejo**, you can park and stroll along the river bank, taking in the **Cathedral** and the restored 19th-century mills known as **Los Molinos del Río** (Plaza de los Molinos, Mon–Sat 11am–2pm, 5–8pm; July and Aug Mon–Fri 10am–2pm, 5–8pm) just below the bridge. For full details of the city, *see page 55*.

The Lower Valley

From the centre of Murcia city, drive south along the road marked for the **Santuario de la Fuensanta** (open daily 9am–1pm, 4–7pm), then turn to follow the right bank of the river, invisible behind rustling fields of sweet corn, sugar-cane and cotton. From **Alquerías** to **Beniel**, you can follow a small farm road between the orchards. If you drive up to the sanctuary at **Orihuela** there is a wonderful view over the sea of mottled greens on the valley floor. Orihuela's old centre *(described in more detail on page 62)* repays leisurely exploration. Take the road down the right bank to Bigastro and **Jacarilla**, where there is a lovely garden around the country house of the **Marqueses de Fontalbá** (Avda de la Cruz s/n; open Tues–Sun 9am–6pm).

From here, it is a straightforward ride back to Guardarmar on the coast.

Above: selling fish at Guardarmar

the south murcia region

18. A MORNING AT A SPA *(see map, p52–53)*

Allow 1 hour by car from Alicante, or 45 minutes from Murcia. The spa is only open in the morning.

Murcia region is something of a paradise for lovers of spa towns, with a choice of nearly half a dozen thermal baths dotted around the countryside. Most have been in continual use since at least Roman times, and remain wonderfully old-fashioned in different ways. This is especially true of two small spas in the Sierra de Espuña: **Fuensanta**, tucked away up a small road into the sierras an hour's drive from Lorca and completely uncommercialised (the waters are recommended for skin treatment); and the baths in the middle of the small town of **Alhama de Murcia** (next to the Parque Cubana; open Mon–Sat 9am–1pm, 4–7pm), which were recently restored for local use and are pleasantly casual.

Closer to Murcia city is **Baños de Mula**, a wonderful spa village nestling in the Mula Valley. Here you can rent rooms or flats with private mineral baths by the hour (€10–18) or overnight for €48–60. It is also possible to have a hydromassage. The tiled patios and baths, the village atmosphere and the bare sunbaked hills all around give the feel of another world lost in time (*see page 94* for reservations).

Archena and Fortuna

Just 20 minutes away from here, sitting on the lush riverside in the Segura valley, are the baths at **Archena**, which knew glory in Roman times and later belonged to the Order of St John of Jerusalem. They are geared up to serious pampering – marble pavements set the tone – and are unbeatable for atmosphere and setting, but are tailored to three-week courses of treatment under medical supervision rather than a lazy morning of self-indulgence. Nonetheless the spa complex now has a year-round swimming pool under a glass bubble for those who want a quick dip in the waters (10am–10.30pm; entrance fee; swimming cap obligatory).

The other spa well worth sampling is **Fortuna**. It is sedately functional rather than elegant, but the outside world drops away once you are immersed in the deep marble baths. The waters themselves are said to be some of the most beneficial in Europe. The treatments – everything from nasal douches, needle showers and water massages to mud baths – are very reasonably priced, so you may want to try a selection. But be warned; since the baths are open in the mornings only it's advisable to telephone in advance (tel: 968 685 011).

If you want to stay in the area for the afternoon, the nearby **Saladar del Ajauque** is noted for its rare plants and profusion of birdlife.

Right: Mula's emblem

19. ORIHUELA AND LORCA *(see map, p52–53)*

Orihuela is a 30–40 minute drive from either Murcia or Alicante. You need a full morning to see its old centre. Allow 2–3 hours to explore Lorca (an hour's drive away).

Everyday life ticks over in Orihuela and Lorca against a backdrop of stunning architecture. Buildings crumble away and priests and farmers go about their daily business apparently unaware of the towns' beauty. This very lack of self-consciousness, the way in which tourism plays second fiddle to local life, gives an added dimension to any visit to these towns.

A Rich Heritage

The old quarter of **Orihuela** (**Oriola**) runs around the left bank of the river under the prow of the sierra. The aged buff-stone provincial shops and backstreets, the palm forest on the edge of town and the crumbling palaces and the glassy river provide the backdrop to the monumental centre.

The town's credentials explain its rich heritage: an independent capital in the 8th century; the launching pad for Ferdinand and Isabella's final assault on Granada in 1492; a wealthy Renaissance university and cathedral city; and later, in the 18th century, commercial focus of the fertile lower Segura valley. Its political power faded only in the early 19th century, when Alicante took over as regional capital and five of its monasteries were dissolved. Today, despite its fame as the birthplace of Miguel Hernández, shepherd and radical poet who died in prison after the Civil War, it remains a deeply conservative *castellano*-speaking town, looking more to the past than the future.

There is space here to describe only a few highlights. Usefully, all now share the same visiting hours (Tues–Sun 10am–2pm, 5–9pm, closing at 8pm Oct–Mar). One is the **Colegio de Santo Domingo**, found on the edge of town – turn immediately right under the arched **Puerta de Crevillente** (called the angels' gate) at the end of the town's palm forest. The proportions of its cloistered patios spell out its importance first as a convent and later as a university (1610–1824). Now it is a private school run by the bishopric. You are unlikely to gain access to the church, but you can see the tiled frieze in the

the south murcia region

former refectory and the panelled and coffered main staircase. The **Casa de Miguel Hernández**, his birthplace, is nearby in Calle Miguel Hernández.

Another highlight is the shadowy **Cathedral**, an inspired small-scale patchwork of styles varying from Romanesque and Catalan Gothic to baroque. Below the vaulting, defined by spiral ribs, there is fine Renaissance ironwork, a rich 17th-century carved choir, an ornate baroque organ and, in the sacristy, Velázquez's wonderful *Temptation of Saint Thomas*. This is only the most famous among many fabulous paintings in the museum (visits to the tower at 11am, 12.30 and 4.30pm). There are many other curiosities too, such as the 16th-century brass Virgen del Cabildo, made for versatility and economy with two detachable heads and pairs of hands to change her character. Opposite the Cathedral, right on the river itself, stands the 17th-century **Palacio Episcopal**, with its very fine cloister.

Further along the river stands the church of **Santas Justa y Rufina**, its gargoyled clock tower marking the southern boundary of Catalan Gothic. Beyond the Renaissance **town hall** and the **Palacio Rubalcaba**, where the tourist office and a good bar are located, is the small underground **Museo de la Muralla** presenting a stretch of the Muslim city's wall and baths in a guided 25-minute tour, and the **Church of Santiago**. Its carved Isabelline portal bears the yoke and arrows of the Catholic kings. Inside, the Gothic austerity is broken by rich altarpieces by Salzillo, the Murcian sculptor whose lyrical realism has come to define Spanish baroque. More of his work can be viewed in the **Museo de Semana Santa** in the Iglesia de la Merced, where the town's *pasos*, processional sculptures for Holy Week, are kept.

Good central eating places serving local food include **Casablanca** (tel: 96 530 1029), in Calle Mecca, and the **Atereo** (tel: 96 530 4018) inside the Casino. Here there is a wonderful combination of the rice so typical of Alicante and vegetables of the Murcian *huerta*.

Faded Beauty

Like Orihuela, **Lorca** is more than the sum of its parts. The old town, running down a gentle slope, is another world, quietly faded in some parts, crumbling away or abandoned in others. It grew up as a Roman highway stop on the Vía Heraklia linking the mines of Jaen to the port of Cartagena. Then it became military capital of Teodomiro's independent Visigothic state of Murcia and later a strongly defended frontier city between Muslim *taifas*. Hence its oldest buildings are civic rather than religious: a Roman mile-

Left: the cathedral cloister at Orihuela
Above: detail, Iglesia de Santiago, Orihuela

stone (originally found in Plaza San Vicente), the 13th-century castle keep and the Porche San Antonio, a medieval city gate.

But, as in Orihuela, the overall feel is Renaissance and baroque, the result of a building splurge after the fall of Granada, when the town was slowly repopulated by Catalans and Aragonese. Close to the central Plaza de España, you will find turrets, elaborate shields, cornices, lanterns and carved doorways decorating Italianate aristocratic houses, the granary and the town hall. **San Patricio**, the largest of the town's churches – so called because Alfonso X took the town from the Moors on St Patrick's day – looms up in lofty splendour behind its baroque façade. Its 17th-century paintings include a black Christ. Among the town's other 10 churches, **San Francisco** particularly merits a look (most are not left open during the day).

Over the past decade, the old town has undergone a major overhaul. Houses are being restored with traditional balconies and *palominas*, or outside hanging larders. It has also become one of the main crafts centres of Spain, with an excellent **Centro Regional de Artesanía** (Mon–Fri 10am–2pm and 4–7.30pm, Sat 11am–1.30pm. 4.30–6.30pm, Sun noon–2pm) built on Calle Lopez de Gisbert, next to the Iglesia San Mateo. Here you can examine the best selection of local crafts in the region, most notably the embroidered silk used to dress the figures of the famous Semana Santa processions and *jarapas* (cotton rugs); these are on show all year round in four small museums run by the main brotherhoods. There is also a good range of ceramics and pottery – clearly Muslim influenced – from the towns of the nearby Sierra de Espuña. A small tourist train, which starts close to the river, links the other main tourist sights; these include the **Museo Arqueologico** (Tues–Sun 10.30am–2pm and 4.30–7.30pm; Apr–Sept 5–8pm) and the Muslim and

Above: Lorca's castle
Left: angel statue in Lorca

Christian **castle**, which is organised like a history theme park, with live performances. For the independently minded, an 8-km (5-mile) walk to the river is signposted from the castle to the Cejo de los Enamorados.

20. THE SIERRAS DE ESPUÑA AND MORATALLA
(see map, p52–53)

A 1½-hour drive from Alicante (45 minutes from Murcia city) takes you to the start of the Sierra de Espuña's pine forests; another hour to the furthest point, Moratalla, and the sierras.

Unlike the Andalucian sierras, the rocky massifs of Murcia have no place in travel literature or the romantic imagination. Yet the mountains, the tail end of the same chain, are quite as beautiful as anything further west, dropping from forested heights to crumpled chalky hills which have kept the architectural stamp of their history as the frontier with Muslim Granada.

This semi-circular route for a two-day foray (but allow three to four for serious walking) starts at **Alhama de Murcia**'s castle ruins and thermal baths. Just beyond, at **Totana**, where flowery glazed ceramics are made, turn off for **Aledo**, stopping off at the sanctuary of **Santa Eulalia** (always open in daylight hours). A small gem with a *mudéjar* coffered ceiling, its 17th-century frescoed cartoons tell the story of a child martyr persecuted by the Romans. Outside is a bar-restaurant. Aledo itself was an important frontier town belonging to the Order of Santiago from the 13th to the 15th centuries, and has tremendous views and the remains of its Muslim **fortress**.

Mountain Sanctuary
A few kilometres along the same road is the entrance to the **Reserva Nacional de Sierra de Espuña**, one of Spain's largest nature reserves. It protects a vast area of pine forest, replanted on bare slopes in the late 19th century to prevent flooding in the villages below, and flora and fauna that includes over 250 plant species, mountain cats, wild boars, native tortoises, white squirrels and rare butterflies.

The eastern exit of the park opens onto the road to **Pliego**, which runs through vineyards, almond and olive groves to meet the main road to **Mula**, a historic small town sheltering under splendidly sited castle ruins (Muslim and restored in the 16th century). It keeps a clutch of churches, traditional potters and aristocratic palaces, one of which houses the **Museo de El Cigarralejo** (Calle del Marqués 1; Tues–Sat 10.30am–2pm, Sun and holidays 10.30am–1pm), a small but stunning museum where you can see the extraordinary finds from a nearby Iberian burial site. Here the dead were buried with their possessions and messages to the gods in large ceramic pots after cremation in a funeral pyre; these funeral trousseaux have allowed

Right: the sanctuary at Santa Eulalia

an unprecedented reconstruction of everyday Iberian life. As the excavations continue, new finds are being added to the museum.

Pilgrimage Site

The road runs west from Mula to Moratalla through **Bullas** (*see page 58*), **Cehegin** and **Caravaca de la Cruz**, which became one of Spain's three official pilgrimage places in 2003 (the others being Santiago de Compostella and the Monastery of Santo Toribio de Liébana in Cantabria). A frontier town from the 11th to the 15th centuries, Caravaca is riddled with medieval mythology woven around the Knights Templar. Inside the **castle** you can see the church window where, it is said, angels flew in with a four-armed cross in front of the Muslim king, who subsequently converted

to Christianity. A bejewelled reproduction of the cross, worshipped here since the 13th century, is kept in the museum (10am–1pm and 4.30–7pm; closed Mon and Sun). During the May fiestas (*see page 85*) it is bathed in wine and water. The hermitage itself has a marble facade influenced by colonial or Latin baroque, splendidly out of context here.

Below the castle, in the old town, wander down the pedestrianised **Calle Mayor**, take a look at the 16th-century **Iglesia de la Concepción** and, if you have time, drive out of town to see the Roman Temple and Bronze Age site at **La Encarnación**. The **Fuentes de el Marqués** is a beauty spot just outside town, with a quiet stretch of river, caves, a nature study centre and a good restaurant.

Romantic Village

Moratalla, the seat of the Order of Santiago for centuries, is a fairy-tale village. Backed by forested slopes, its streets wind up, as if around a snail's shell, to the 14th-century castle (the key, said to be the original, and torch for the dark tower, are kept at a nearby house). From here, there are splendid views over the fruit orchards and folded hills.

From Moratalla the road to the **Ermita Rogativa** will take you into the highest land of the province, populated only by scattered *cortijos*, or farmhouses in the Andalucian style. Much wildlife remains and, if you take binoculars and are lucky, you may see some of the Iberian peninsula's last herds of mountain goats.

If you have a third day, you could stay overnight in Moratalla and take the road down to **Lorca** (*see page 63*), turning off at **La Paca** to see the Argaric village at **Coy** and/or, just before you get into Lorca, the famous dams of **Puentes** and **Valdeinfierno**, built in the 18th century. The herby scrubland here is good walking country and from Lorca it is a quick drive back to Murcia city.

Above: mountains above Moratalla

21. CARTAGENA CITY *(see map, p52–53)*

A morning in Cartagena's museums and old town can be extended with a trip through mining country to an unspoilt beach.

Cartagena is one of the most frustrating of all historic cities. Its site, one of the safest natural harbours of the Mediterranean, speaks of its past greatness, and untold archaeological riches lie below its modern bourgeois overcoat. For an entire millennium, this was a key Mediterranean metropolis under the control of the Iberians, Phoenicians, Greeks, Carthaginians and Romans in turn. 'New Carthage is by far the most powerful of all the cities in this country,' wrote Strabo, the Roman historian, 'adorned by secure fortifications, by walls handsomely built, by harbours, by a lake and by the silver mines…'

Yet this very wealth of resources and strategic siting made the city too desirable for its own good. Stripped of its forest by the Carthaginians and Romans in order to supply fuel for the mines – Hasdrubal, Hannibal's brother extracted 300lb of silver a day – and razed to the ground in the 7th century by the Visigothic king Sisebuto, it never found the same glory again. Many of its great buildings were used as quarries in later centuries and, to add insult to injury, wartime battering and defensive rebuilding have, over the centuries, eroded the traces of its past.

Hence today the city is initially unprepossessing, dominated by naval dockyards, modern development and industry. Around the corner, at Escombreras, is the largest oil refinery in Spain. But the historic core of the city and harbour area is gradually being revealed under the ramshackle streets built over it in later centuries. Even so there is much work to be done; the Roman Capitol lies under a grassy hillock (the Molinete).

City Sights

A good place to start is the ruined **Castillo de la Concepción** (open daily 10am–6.30pm, may close summer lunchtimes), the Roman castle, above the magnificent harbour spread below. To the north lie the bullring, built over

Above: children playing in Cartagena

the Roman amphitheatre (currently being excavated), and the naval hospital, now a university. From the castle you can walk down into town past the ruined **Catedral Antigua**, thought to be one of the oldest churches in Spain and has a Roman mosaic in the crypt, and the **Roman theatre**, discovered in 1987 and now almost entirely excavated (both open Mon–Sun 10.30am–1.30pm, 6–8pm, summer 5–7pm). Nearby is the **Byzantine Wall**, on show under an excellent contemporary art gallery (corner of Calle Dr Tapia and C. de la Soledad), while a newer excavation, this time of a Roman street, can be seen under Calle Duque 29 and neighbouring buildings (open during banking hours; free). However, the most important Roman monument is the newly excavated **Augusteum**, a splendid early temple (C. Cabellero 2; Tues–Sun 10am–2pm, 3–6.30pm). Guided tours are available to all these and other Roman, Punic or Byzantine sites; enquire at the tourist office.

The **Museo Nacional de Arqueología Marítima** (Dique de Navidad; Tues–Sat 9am–3pm, Sun 10am–3pm, closed holidays) houses finds from shipwrecked boats, and a full-scale replica of a Roman galley. The **Museo Arqueológico Municipal** (Calle Ramón y Cajal 45; Tues–Fri 10am–2pm, 5–8pm, weekends 11am–2pm), built over an important necropolis, has an excellent collection that reflects the long overlap between Iberian and Roman cultures. Smaller naval and artillery museums are pointers to the city's continuing role as a naval and military base.

Modernist Architecture

Cartagena's other strong suit is wonderful Modernist (art deco) architecture, paid for by mining wealth. Most of it dates from the years 1895–97 when a new grid of streets was laid out. What survives is clustered along the axis of the Calle Mayor: the **town hall**, the splendid **Casino**, and the **Casas Cervantes**, Pedreno and Llagostera. The **Gran Hotel** and house at No. **27** on

Calle Jara, the **Palacio de Aguirre** in the **Plaza de Merced**, and the **train station** are other good examples. These Modernist buildings, and tombs in the splendid cemetery of **Nuestra Señora de los Remedios**, are heavy with allegory and symbolism. Much of it is said to be Masonic – handed down from the mysterious Knights Templar.

The pedestrianised heart of the old town has wonderful old-fashioned shops and lots of atmospheric bars and restaurants such as **Columbus** at Calle Mayor 18, **La Casa Tomas**, Plaza Lopez Pinto 8, or **La Tartana** *(see page 76)*. Afterwards, the drive eastward past the mines towards **Cabo de Palos** can be linked with a trip to the unspoilt beach at **Calblanque** *(see page 69)*.

Left: Modernista (art deco) architecture in Cartagena

22. LA UNION, CALBLANQUE AND CABO DE PALOS
(see map, p52–53)

The road east from Cartagena travels through beautiful country to Calblanque, a natural park enclosing virgin beaches, salt lakes and rocky heights. Cabo de Palos has fish restaurants and a marine reserve.

The highway running east from Cartagena to the **Mar Menor** would never suggest the wild sierra and coastal landscapes lying just to the south. In the distance floats the highrise horizon of La Manga, the sandbar which encloses the Mar Menor, or 'small sea'.

But just a few kilometres away, the road to Portman takes you into another world. In the empty, beautiful ochre and tawny hills that run down to the **Portman**, the Phoenicians, Romans and 19th-century fortune hunters drew huge wealth from silver, lead and gold mines. Today all that remains are the mining chimneys and old-fashioned machinery down by the silted up port, called Portus Magnus by the Romans. Although dumping was halted in 1990, a final solution has not yet been found to clean the shoreline. Nonetheless the bay, overlooked by its lighthouse, has its own rugged beauty.

Inland at **La Unión**, the small 19th-century capital of the mining country, Modernist buildings include the **Antiguo Mercado Publico**, the venue for an annual festival dedicated to the mining flamenco that grew up here among the Andalucian workers (*see page 85*). The **Museo Minero** housed in the 19th-century Liceo de Obreros (or Workers' Lycée) explains the mineralogy, history and mining processes used here for over a thousand years (Pl del Piceo s/n; Tues–Fri 10am–1.30pm, 5.30–7.30pm, Sat, Sun and July and Aug am only). The museum also organises visits to Portman's Roman mosaics.

The next turning as you head east on the highway leads to **Calblanque**, a 250-km natural park that contains gloriously unspoiled sandy and rocky bays. There is an information centre close to the park's entrance.

To the Cape

At weekends locals stream past here to the fish restaurants (*see page 75*) at **Cabo de Palos**, a small village with old-fashioned villas clustered around fishing boats bobbing in the port. The main speciality here is *calderó*, the local fishermen's meal of rice cooked in stock followed by a plateful of fish baked in a salt crust. Today the off-shore waters are protected as a Marine Reserve with access for diving by special permission only (tel: 968 228 918).

For those who prefer to stay above the water, there are tailor-made boat trips to the Islas Pedrigueras, in the enclosed Mar Menor, from various beaches, including Cabo de Palos and La Manga, during the summer months.

Right: fishing remains an important industry in the Mar Menor

the south murcia region

Leisure
Activities

SHOPPING

Spain is no longer the budget holiday destination it once was, so do not expect to find lots of dirt-cheap bargains. However, locally manufactured items such as clothes, shoes and leather goods tend to be of very good quality.

The coast itself is not abundantly rich in local crafts, and those that do exist are now being gradually squeezed out by the advent of mass production. Nevertheless, there is an enticing array of local food and wine to be had. Inland areas, especially Murcia, have maintained their often Muslim-influenced crafts traditions, and they provide the most interesting souvenirs.

Most shops are open Mon–Fri 10am–1.30pm, 5–8pm, Sat 10am–1.30pm. Some bakeries and newsagents also open for a few hours on Sunday mornings. Department stores, hypermarkets and big supermarkets stay open during the siesta, so this is a good time to shop if you want to avoid the crowds.

Markets

All neighbourhoods in Spain have municipal food markets (*mercados,* 8.20am–1.30 or 2pm), which are often the best places to buy fresh produce. General street markets (*mercadillos*), found in nearly every resort, are best for buying items such as rope-soled sandals (*alpargatas*), relatively cheap clothing, household goods such as *paella* pans, etc.

Murcia also has travelling craft markets that move from town to town on Sundays.

Alicante/Alacant

Thur, Sat, 8am–2pm. Campoamor (near Pl. de Toros). Street market ranging from fruit and vegetables to clothes.
Daily, particularly evenings. Explanado de España. Particularly good for jewellery, leather goods, cheap watches, etc.

Left: produce of the plains
Right: fish is a local staple

Altea

Tues, 8am–1.30pm. By the port. Very tourist-orientated; cheap jeans, pearls from Mallorca, etc. A few local goods.

Calpe

Mon–Fri, 5–7.30pm. Electronic fish market – a lot of fun because it's fast and exciting, like a stock exchange.

Dénia

Mon, 8am–2pm. By the railway station. Almonds, raisins, fig cake, etc.

Játiva/Xàtiva

Tues, Thur mornings. Pl. del Mercat. A good mixture of small stalls of the kind you would find in an inland, market town.

Murcia

Daily. Pl. de las Flores. Flower market.
Dec. Christmas crafts, including wooden nativity figures (Avda Alfonso XII).

Santa Pola

Tues–Sat, 5–6pm. At the port. Auction of fresh fish direct from the boats. Stalls outside also sell fish in small quantities.

Torrevieja
Fri. Huge street market.

Mainstream shopping
High-street fashion and department stores are clustered in the towns' main central shopping streets, as follows: **Alicante**, Avda Maisonnare; **Elche**, C. de la Corredera; **Murcia**, Gran Vía Escaltor Salzillo and Jabonerías; **Benidorm**, C. Rambo and Avda Mediterraneo; **Lorca**, C. Corredera; **Denia**, C. Mqués de Campo, **Torrevieja** C. Ramongallud.

Local Crafts and Products
The following towns are known for particular local products: **Abarán**, *esparto* grass mats; **Agost**, pottery; **Alcoi**, sugar-coated almonds; **Crevillente**, glassware, rugs and carpets, wickerwork and *esparto* grass; **Dénia**, raisins; **Elche**, shoes; **Elda**, shoes and lace; **Gata de Gorgos**, cane and basket work; **Guadalest**, leather goods, shawls, lace work; **Ibi**, toys; **Jijona**, *turrón*; **Murcia city**, carved figurines; **Valencia city**, fans; **Villajoyosa**, chocolate. **Lorca** hosts a fair of regional crafts in September.

Agost
Pottery: Museo d'Alfarería, C. Teulería 11, tel: 96 509 1199. Closed Mon. Good range, with pots from Biar. At the Tibi entrance to town are **Hermanos Molla** (traditional functional items) and **Emili Boix** (decorative, modern ceramics). All of these sell traditional white earthenware water bottles (*botijos*).

Alicante/Alacant
Ceramics: V. Pascual, Avda. Alfonso X El Sabio 15, tel: 96 514 0139. Pottery and crafts. **Turrón: Turrones Teclo**, C. Mayor 23, tel: 96 520 1115. *Turrón*, chocolate, wines and dates, plus other local produce. **Cartegena: Centro Regional de la Artesanía**, C. Honda 10, tel: 968 524 631.

Elche/Elx
Shoes: Salvador Artesano, Carr. Murcia-Alicante km 53, tel: 96 667 5441 (Mon–Sat 9am–1.30pm, 3.30–9pm). You can watch the shoes being made. There are other factory outlets nearby on the N340 to Crevillente.

Gata de Gorgos
Cane and Wickerwork: A string of shops selling furniture, baskets and mats. **Guitars: Guitarras Cashimira**, C. Estación 25. Medium quality guitars.

Jalón/Xaló
Wine: Bodega Cooperativa Virgen Pobre, Carr. Xaló–Alacalí s/n, tel: 96 648 0034. Excellent for reds, rosés and sweet *mistela*, raisins and olive oil. Mon–Fri and Sun mornings.

Jijona/Xixona
Turrón: Museo de Turrón El Lobo, Ctra de Busot 1, tel: 96 561 0225.

Jumilla
Wine: Bodegas San Isidro, Carr. de Murcia s/n (on road to Yecla at La Alquería), tel: 968 780 700. Mon–Sat 8am–1.30pm, 3.30–7pm. Best known for red wines.

Lorca
Crafts: Centro Regional de Artesanía, C. Lope Gisbert s/n, tel: 968 463 912. Permanent exhibition hall, with two areas for temporary displays as well as interesting archives of local crafts. **Embroidery: Joaquín Castellar**, C. Corredera 35. Workshop based on local tradition of lace and embroidery. **Pottery: Lario Marin**, Carretera Murcia 23, tel: 968 468 183.

Murcia
Carved figurines (*belenes*): **Manuel Nicolás Almansa**, C. Belenes 12, Santiago el Mayor, tel: 968 255 858 **Artesanía Hnos. Griñán**, C. del Amistad 10, Puente Tocinos, tel: 968 302 211 These are two of 12 or so *belén*-makers still working in the studio. **Crafts: Centro Regional de Artesanía**, C. Actor Francisco Rabal 8, tel: 968 284 585. Fine cooperative for local crafts at workshop prices.

Villajoyosa/La Vila Joiosa
Chocolate: Chocolatería Valor, Avda. País Valencia 10, tel: 96 589 4099. Buy solid chocolate to take away, or stay for the ultimate hot chocolate and *churros*.

Right: *arroz abanda* – the fisherman's favourite

EATING & DRINKING

Local Cuisine and Produce

On the fertile plains backing the Costa Blanca, the wide range of local produce – oranges and lemons, almonds, rice, a huge range of vegetables, wonderful fish and game – makes for varied, sensual and colourful Mediterranean cooking. Lighter than Catalan cuisine, it carries a southern air with a subtly spiced trail of Muslim influences.

Good regional cooking here remains largely traditional, so there is no need to look for named restaurants. On the other hand, if you are looking for a special meal, there is a new young generation of chefs serving local *alta cocina*.

Paella, which originated in Valencia as poor country food made with rabbit and snails, is the most famous local dish, but it is only one in a vast family of *arroces* (rices). Don't be put off by humbler combinations – they can be the most delicious. From the coast come *arroz abanda* and *caldero*, both made with stock from the small rock fish that fishermen could not sell in the old days; on the plains, vegetables and pork products flavour various *paella huertanos* and *arroz con costra*; in the mountains, *arroces serranos* are typically flavoured with snails, herbs from the sierras and local game such as rabbit.

Fish dishes are widely available inland, but are usually at their best in ports. Dénia's monster prawns and *arroz abanda*, Santa Pola's *gazpachos de mero*, a fish stew served on flatbread, Cabo de Palo's salt-baked fish and grey mullets' roe (*huevos de mújol* – a Mediterranean caviar) – all gain from on-the-spot freshness and local know-how. Shellfish is generally good, but falling catches have sent prices sky-high. Guardamar's *langostinos*, for example, can cost up to £50 a kilo. These days genuine *salazones* or salted fish products such as *mojama* (salted tuna) and *huevas* (roe), products of a tradition that goes back to Phoenician times, have become luxuries.

Inland, traditional cooking tends to have more Castilian than Mediterranean influences. Humble dishes such as the *migas* based on breadcrumbs, *gazpachos*, shepherds' game-and-poultry stews served on top of a flat bread (which originally served as the plate) and *trigo picado*, a cracked wheat stew, are increasingly appreciated as gourmet dishes.

In the Alicante mountains, the cuisine becomes more warming: soups, stews *(ollas)* and other dishes based on dried beans, *bacalao* (salt-cod) or cured meats, cooked with saffron and the herbs of the sierras. The most famous of these are *olleta* and *giraboix*, and *pericana*, griddled salt-cod seasoned with dried peppers, garlic and olive oil.

There is plenty of variety when it comes to picnic food too: local fresh and cured goat's milk cheeses, various types of cured *chorzo* (sausage with paprika), jamón and other charcuterie. In Alicante, *coques*, first cousins to Italian pizzas, use the same Mediterranean vegetables on crispy, thin pastry crusts. Also typical of the *huertas* are sausages made with sweet pork and

poultry fattened on fruit and corn, *paste-les* (meat pies), and honey from the Ali-cante orange groves.

As rice is to savoury dishes, so oranges, lemons and almonds are to sweets. Oranges and lemons appear in huge mounds on road-side stalls (only buy in season), in fruit tarts and as glacé fruit. Almonds are frequently used in cakes, biscuits, puddings, liqueurs and sweets. *Turrón* nougat is wolfed down by the locals in great quantities at Christmas, and candied egg yolks *(yemas)* are also very popular.

Refreshing summer drinks and ices are other local specialities that, like many local traditions, are said to be a legacy from Islamic times. For the best ice cream, a *granizado* (icy slush made from lemon, orange or coffee) or *horchata* (a milky, semi-frozen made from ground tiger nuts, plus sugar and water), look for words *fabricación propia* or *artesanal* (handmade) on the sign.

Regional Wines

The most prestigious vineyard areas – Monóvar and Gorgos valley in Alicante; Jumilla, Yecla and Bullas in Murcia – are strong on robust country dishes which complement their wines. The best Alicante, Jumilla and Valencia DO (Denomination of Origin) wines are rising stars – reasonably priced and influenced by New World styles and organic growing methods.

For good local wines, or *vinos del país,*

which can be found in most restaurants, see the chapters with the relevant itineraries and options.

Eating Out

Eating out is cheap, varied and cosmopolitan near the coast. The selection of places under Recommended Restaurants concentrates on good local cooking.

Complaints: As is the case in many hotels, restaurants here often make a complaints book available for comments by dissatisfied customers.

Opening Times: Holidays and closing times vary. A lot of restaurants that are not in or near major tourist centres are closed on Sunday evenings (or even all day in city centres) and for one weekday and one to two months during the summer or autumn. Phone in advance to check that your choice of eatery is open. Standard kitchen hours are 1pm–4pm and 7.30pm–midnight (occasionally until 11pm).

Most Spaniards do not eat lunch until 2pm; and dinner until 10pm, but restaurants in tourist centres are accustomed to people eating earlier than this and have adjusted their times accordingly.

Payment/Tips: Prices may or may not include IVA (VAT), so check the menu; either way it is common practice to leave a 10 percent tip if you are happy with the meal and the service.

Restaurant Grading: Restaurants are graded in four classes (plus de luxe), but the grading often refers to the decor, the number of dishes on the menu and the price of the set tourist menu, rather than the quality of the food and service.

Snacks: If you want a light meal, many bars and *cervecerías* serve a selection of *tapas* (small dishes of tasty snacks eaten with a drink). They come in three sizes: *pinchos* (a mouthful, traditionally offered free but now more usually at a price), *tapas* (enough to fill a saucer), and *raciones* (a small plateful). You pay when you have finished rather than after each item.

Vegetarians: Meat and fish tend to dominate Spanish menus, but in almost all restaurants you will be able to get a plain *tortilla* and salad, or a selection of vegetable *tapas*, such as broad beans, roasted

Left: a selection of *tapas*

aubergines, fennel. Three recommendations for vegetarians are: El Girasol, Calle San José 22, Murcia, tel: 968 212 965 and, in Alicante, L'Indret, Calle García Morato 5, Alicante, tel: 96 521 6614, and Biomenu, Navas 17, tel: 96 521 3144.

Recommended Restaurants

Restaurant prices are graded as follows:

$ – Inexpensive
$$ – Moderate
$$$ – Expensive

Agres (northern Alicante)
Pensión Mariola
C. San Antonio 4
Tel: 96 551 0017
Large dining room. Provides excellent country cooking. Also offers a hostal, with flats. Closed 1–15 July, 1–15 Oct. MC, DC, V. $-$$

Alhama de Murcia (central Murcia)
El Chaleco
Avda de Bastarrecte 9
Tel: 968 630 104
Modern and traditional dishes served in a sleek, sophisticated setting. Closed for two weeks in Aug. $$$

Alicante/Alacant (city)
Dársena
Muelle de Levante 6
Tel: 96 520 7399 / 520 7589
A great place to sample the region's rice dishes, fish and shellfish. More relaxed during the evening than at lunchtime, when it can be hectic. Closed Sun evenings, Mon in summer and 15–27 Jan. MC, DC,V, AM. $$$

La Goleta
Explanada de España 8
Tel: 96 521 4392
Seafood and rice on the seafront. MC, DC, V AM. $$

Nou Manolín
C. Villegas 3
Tel: 96 520 0368
This is the place to experience creative regional cooking, and some great wines. MC, DC, V, AM. $$-$$$

Alteá (central Alicante)
La Capella
San Pablo 1
Tel: 96 688 0484
Well-cooked traditional cooking with modern influences. Has an attractive open-air terrace. $$

Bañeres (southern Alicante)
Venta El Borrego
Ctra Villena-Ontenienle km18
Tel: 96 656 7457
Traditional inn specialising in herby mountain *gazpachos* to order and tasty game stews. MC, DC, V, AM. $

Benidorm (central Alicante)
La Rana
Costera del Barco s/n
Casa Antig (or smaller branch at La Raneta, C. Martinez Oriola 25)
Tel: 96 586 8120
Specialises in genuine, good *tapas* using high quality fresh produce that can be eaten on their own or combined to make a satisfying meal. Has a very central location. MC, DC, V, AM. $-$$

El Molino
Ctra Valencia km123
Tel: 96 585 7181
Ambience of a traditional inn and offering good food and a summer terrace. Open all year, including fiestas, when many other restauants are closed. MC, DC, V, AM. $$-$$$

Ulía
Pº Mantimo s/n, La Cala
Tel: 96 585 6828
Tasty local rice dishes and fresh fish cooked and served on the beach. MC, V. $$

Cabo de Palos (central Murcia)
La Tana
Paseo de la Barra 33
Tel: 968 563 003
La Tana is especially recommended for its sea bass baked in salt, the house speciality. Closed Mon, except in summer, and Nov. MC, DC, V, AM. $$

Cartagena (Murcia)
La Tartana
Puerta de Murcia 14
Tel: 968 500 011
Modern regional cooking in the form of lunches, suppers and tapas. Located just outside the old town. Closed Sun and summer. DC, V. $–$$

Castalla (southern Alicante)
Mesón El Viscayo
Camino La Bola s/n
Tel: 96 556 0196
The house specialities include tasty mountain *gazpachos* and home-made breads. Set meal format. Open lunches only and Sat pm. MC, DC, V. $

Cocentaina (northern Alicante)
La Escaleta
Pujada Estació del Nord 205
Tel: 96 559 2100
Creative Michelin-starred regional cooking. Closed Sun pm, Mon, Easter. AE, MC, DC, V. $$

Dénia
El Pegolí
Baret de Les Rotes
Tel: 96 578 1035
Family restaurant featuring a set menu of giant prawns, *arroz aband*a and fresh fruit, or fish and shellfish. If El Pegolí is full, you could try El Trampoli or Mesón Troya, which are also good. Closed Mon and for three weeks over the Christmas period. V. $$$

El Poblet
Las Mannas km 2.5, Urb El Poblet
Tel: 96 578 4179
This is considered Alicante's best restaurant for haute cuisine; Quique Dacosta's cooking is worth the extra expense. Closed Sun pm, Mon. AE, MC, V. $$$

El Algar (Murcia coast)
Los Churrascos
Avda Filipinas 13
Tel: 968 136 144
A great place to sample good regional cooking. $$–$$$

Elche/Elx
Mesón El Granaino
Josep María Buch 40
Tel: 96 666 4080
Great *tapas* and local dishes such as *arroz con costra* (rice with egg crust). Closed Sun and most of August. AE, MC, DC, V. $$

Játiva/Xàtiva (Valencia)
Fonda Casa Floro
Pl. del Mercat 46
Tel: 96 227 3020
Good home cooking, including *Arroz al horno* and *gazpachos*. Packed on market days. Lunch only. Closed Aug. $. For dinner try La Abnela, which is also good. $$$

Jumilla (north Murcia)
Casa Sebastián
Mercado de Abastos
Avda3. de Levante 6
Tel: 968 780 194
Breakfast and lunch are served until 4.15pm. Robust regional cooking complements a selection of excellent wine (the cellar is reputed to containts some 18,000 bottles). Closed last two weeks in Aug, Sun and hols. $–$$

Lorca (southwest Murcia)
Cándido
Sto Domingo 13
Tel: 968 466 907
Country fare. 365 days. MC, DC, V. $

Mazarrón (south Murcia)
Virgen del Mar
P^O Maritimo s/n
Tel: 968 595 057
Delicious home cooking based on the fish of the day and local seasonal vegetables. It is usually very busy, so get there early or book. Closed Nov. $

Puertos de Santa Barbara (Cartagena)
María Zapata
Paraje Rupatos s/n
Tel: 968 163 030
Excellent menu of local dishes, home-made cheese and home-grown vegetables. Good wine list. Closed Sun eves and Mon. MC, DC, V. $$

Moraiva
La Seu
Dr Calatayud 24
Tel: 96 594 5757
Creative Mediterranean cooking,. Closed Tues, Christmas and 31 Dec–mid Jan. $$$

Murcia (city)
El Condestable
C. Condestable 1
Tel: 968 282 929
Pablo González's cooking recreates and lightens traditional Murcian food. Good local wines. Closed Sun and Aug. $$

El Churra
Avda Maqués de los Vélez 12
Tel: 238 400
Good-value regional cusine. MC, DC, V. $$

El Corral de Jose Luis
Pl. Santo Domingo 14–15
Tel: 968 214 597
Good value central restaurant with a wide range of local *tapas* and sit-down meals.$$

El Rincón de Pepe
Plaza Apóstoles 34
Tel: 968 212 239
Murcian specialities. Closed Sun eves. MC, DC, V, AM. $$–$$$

Ondara (northern Alicante)
Casa Pepa
Partida Parrus 7–30
Tel: 965 766 606
Renowned country restaurant with inspirational cooking. Closed Sun pm, Mon and Feb. Summer lunches only. AE, MC, V. $$$

Pinoso (southern Alicante)
Palo
San Francisco 2
Tel: 96 547 8023
Country restaurant known for its *arroz serrano*, with white snails and rabbit. Closed Aug. MC, DC, V, AM. $$–$$$

Santa Pola
Batiste
Peréz Ojeda 6
Tel: 96 541 1485
Classic restaurant overlooking the harbour with excellent seafood dishes and a tasting menu. Closed Sun eves. AE, MC, DC, V. $$–$$$

Mesón del Puerto
Pérez Ojeda 31
Tel: 96 541 1289
Good value everyday fish establishment, with *gazpachos de mero* – fish stew served on flatbread. Closed mid-Dec–mid-Jan. MC, DC, V, AM. $$

Tàrberna (northern Alicante)
Casa Pinet
Plaza Mayor
Tel: 96 588 4229
Country cooking in a lighthearted political ambience. Excellent *olla*. $

Torrevieja (southern Alicante)
Las Canàs
San Policarpo 13
Tel: 96 571 5248
Popular for fish, seafood and rice. Good value. Closed for two weeks in May and two weeks at Christmas. MC, DC, V, AM $–$$$

Miramar
Po Vista Alegre s/n
Tel: 965 571 3415
Classic waterfront eatery with seafood, fish baked in salt and rice. Closed Nov and Tues Oct–Mar. MC, DC, V, AM. $$–$$$

Villajoyosa/La Vila Joiosa
Hugar del Pescador
Avda País Valencià 33
Tel: 965 890 021
Excellent family fish, seafood and rice restaurant. Closed Mon, dinners only Fri, Sat and Aug. $$$

Right: lunch with an overview

NIGHTLIFE

When night falls, the Costa Blanca and Costa Cálida have something to offer everyone, and there is enough entertainment to keep you going all night in summer and on winter weekends. In addition, there are numerous local fiestas all year round.

Discos, Pubs and Bars

Discos and Spanish-style pubs get going around midnight, and some stay open until breakfast time, so make sure you have a good siesta. Dress is usually casual, but you might well be sent home to change into something more formal if you turn up in shorts.

'Pubs', which are nothing like English pubs and are best described as middle-of-the-road bars, don't have entrance fees, and during the week you probably won't have to pay to get into discos either (especially if you're female). However, at weekends there may be an entrance fee. Drinks in both discos and pubs are pricey, but spirit measures are large.

Bars are open from breakfast time until the early hours of the morning. It is usually cheaper to sit at the bar than at a table.

Alicante, Benidorm, Torrevieja, Lo Pagán and Murcia are the liveliest nightspots.

Alicante/Alacant

During summer, the action is in **San Juan** as well as Alicante itself. Wander along the seafront market (6pm–2am) and enjoy the cafés. **Penelope** is a classic discotheque. Other pubs offer pop music, videos, swimming pools, game machines and pool tables. **Night Fever** is the most popular disco with the under-25s. The municipal Plataforma Cultural is an open-air stage for live music that is open throughout the summer.

For a summer night's entertainment with a more native flavour, start with a drink on the **Explanada**, and then go to Alicante's old town near the cathedral. This is where the bars are concentrated. **La Misión**, **Hanoi 27** and **Nazca** have rooftop terraces. You can listen to good jazz music in stylish **Desafinado** (just off the Rambla) or admire the imaginative décor in **El Forat**. Across the Rambla, **Calle San Fernando** has a host of young people's clubs. **Swing**, by the town hall, is a classic Latino dance venue.

Other alternatives include slick bars such as **Di Roma** and the modern complexes at either end of the harbour, **Birlos**, a disco with show in C. Gerona off the Ramblas, and **Z-Club** for techno (C. Gabriel Miró). **Panoramis,** on the southern wharf, is open 365 days a year.

Benidorm

In summer, every night is party night; in the winter, Benidorm really comes alive only at weekends. The old pedestrian quarter is the scene of many bars and cafés. The main central disco is **Black Sunset** (Calle Esperanto s/n). From the old town young

Above: all-night partying in Alicante only

Spaniards move on to the Paseo de La Playa de Levante, with a cluster of pubs, and from there to the area out of town on the N332. You cannot fail to miss **Ku** (open summer only), a 'spaceship' equipped with bars, disco, helicopter and swimming pool. Avoid **Penélope** – the biggest disco in town – and **KM**, unless you enjoy 'Miss Topless' and 'Miss *Camiseta Mojada*' (wet T-shirt) competitions and other entertainment designed to appeal to the package tourist. Back in town, **Conuco** (Avda Europa) offers salsa dancing – with classes too – and there is also square and sequence dancing, tangos and *copla* in many hotels.

A little further towards Valencia, just after Racó de l'Oix, a discreet signpost announces **L'Anouer** (open all year), a small, up-market bar with roguish churchy-baroque décor, music and a romantic garden.

San Javier and Lo Pagan

The summer resorts here have become a new nightlife centre: **Sal Gorda**, in Santiago de la Ribera, is a good café at which to start the night. The clubs – **El Barracón**, **Apalache** and **Pasaje** – are located in the street behind the church and are open midnight–5am while **Sirocco** in Lo Pagan has good live music on Thurs and Fri. The main discotheque area is on the road to San Pedro del Pinatar.

Murcia city

In the cathedral area, **El Ahorcado Feliz** and **La Puerta Falsa** (for live music) are good bars; **Rincón Latino** is good for live and recorded Latin music (c. Acisido Díaz). **Los Atalayas**, on the road to Alicante, is another nightlife area. **Mundalca** is a classic club-disco opening at 6am (Ctra Sta Catalina s/n).

Torrevieja

In the summer, open air cafés and ice cream parlours fill the streets around the port; later the bars and clubs around the C. del Mar open. Various pavement artists, a funfair and a market (summer, 7pm–1am) add colourful characters. Classic bars, apart from the Casino in the port, are the **Casablanca** and **María Sarmiento**. In winter, Torrevieja is busy only at weekends.

Other places

On the coast, **Altea's** old quarter and beach avenue are full of bars and restaurants. **La Plaza**, next to the church, has live music on Thurs. **Birimbao** and **El Passat-xe** are other popular bars. In both **Calpe** and **Dénia**, the action takes place along the beach – winter weekends and summer only. The busiest area in **Cartagena** is the **Cuesta de la Baronesa** (near the cathedral), where there are many pubs and cafés; other areas include the **Calle Cuatro Santos** and **Calle Bodegones**. In **Santa Pola**, the bars in the town centre (near the port) cater mainly for the younger generation. Among the good discos are **Camelot**, **El Cano** and **Bolero**.

Elche's entertainment is situated in the heart of the town with good live music at **Rompeolas**, whereas **Orihuela's** is practically non-existent. **Alcoi** is generally pretty dead in July and Aug, but the **Santa Rosa** district and also the area around the **Pl. España** perk up in autumn.

Shows and Caberet

For glorious tackiness, you can't beat the expensive extravaganza at the mock castle, **Castillo Conde de Alfaz**, tel: 966 865 592, 7kms (4 miles) from Benidorm just off the N332 to Altea. A mediocre medieval banquet features jousting and duelling (daily; Fri–Sat only). The chamber of horrors leads up to a futuristic disco with its multiple video screens and lasers.

Benidorm Palace, tel: 965 851 660, on the eastern outskirts of town, is reminiscent of a tacky show hall. Catering with a vengeance for the international crowd, it offers 'Spanish style' cabaret and the occasional one-off concert (Julio Iglesias started his career here).

Casinos

You won't de admitted without showing your passport (minimum age 18). Dress is casually smart. The casinos are used to informal tourists and do not have a strict dress code. **Benidorm**: **Casino Mediterraneo** (tel: 965 890 700), 5kms (3 miles) from Benidorm on the N332 towards La Vila Joiosa, open all year 8pm–4am; entrance fee; drinks at pub prices. Games featured include blackjack, *chemin de fer* and roulette. Cash dispenser

Many towns have a **Casa de Cultura**, where concerts and other cultural events takes place. The local savings banks also have auditoriums that host a variety of events. *See also page 85, Festivals.*

Most musical performances are grouped in seasons or festivals; the most important of these are Alicante city's **Festival de Verano** (open-air music, dance and theatre; July–Aug), the **International Jazz Festival** in Murcia (the week after Easter) and **La Mar de Musicas** open-air world music festival in Cartagena (July).

Zambra, a *tablao* in Campello, hosts the province's best year-round **flamenco** shows (Saturdays only in winter, tel: 965 632 310).

in the foyer for credit cards and Eurocheques. Good restaurants.

Murcia: There is a luxury casino in Calle Apóstoles 34.

The Gay Scene

The main centre is **Benidorm**, which has everything from exclusive hotels such as **Villa de los Sueños**, Ctra de Firestraat (tel: 96 586 88 24), through a string of restaurants, saunas and bars for a mainly gay clientèle, although heterosexuals might enjoy the relaxed atmosphere.

Recommended restaurants include **Hierbas** and **Secret Garden**; a bar tour could include **People, Mercury, Orpheo's** and **The Look**. A good starting point in Alicante is **Canibal Shop**, Colón 16, a book, clothes and perfume shop; **La Misión** is a good restaurant, and bars include **Missing** and **La Cúpula Azul**. Venues in Murcia include the **Piscis** bar and **Metropol** club. In **La Manga**, **Papagays** (Ctro Comercial Las Dunas) is the main gay bar.

For Culture Vultures

Theatre and concerts: There are three theatres in **Alcoi**, two of which also show films. All are in or near the **Pl. de España**. Elche and **Murcia** each have one theatre, of which the more important and lively is the **Teatro Romea** in Murcia. Murcia also has good concerts year round in the Auditorio (Avda 1ro Mayo).

Cinemas

There are cinemas in the large towns, as well as summer open-air and drive-in cinemas in the coastal resorts. The **Astoria**, in Alicante's old town (Pl del Carmen 16), occasionally shows subtitled English or other language films in the original print. Many cinemas offer cheap tickets on a particular night of the week.

Bullfighting

Spaniards themselves discuss whether this is a sport, a stylised art form or a barbarian form of torture. You will have to decide whether the sight of a bull being gradually weakened for the kill is for you.

The standard of bullfighting in the region is considered acceptable in **Alicante** (the best time is at the end of June) and **Ondara** *(see page 23)*. There are other bullrings in **Benidorm**, **Cartagena**, **Murcia** (best in the first week of September) and **Torrevieja**, as well as temporary rings in other tourist centres which feature displays by junior *toreros*.

Ticket prices vary considerably between and within each bullring. It is definitely worth paying the extra to sit in the shade during the summer and also to hire a cushion, because the spectacle lasts 2½ hours or more, which can be unbearable in the hot sun. Be aware that an agency will charge up to 20 percent more than the standard price for a ticket, and a hotel will charge up to 40 percent more.

Above: fluent in body language
Right: for aquatic thrills and spills, take your pick from one of five coastal water parks

SPORTS & ACTIVITIES

For Children and the Young at Heart

There are three **water parks** along the coast (at Benidorm, Torrevieja and Rojales), where you can spend a day sliding and splashing about. Take sensible precautions against accidents – fatalities have been known to happen at water parks.

Local **boat rides** go from Jávea (Jun–Sept), Calpe (around the Peñon d'Ifach, summer only), Benidorm (to the island, all year) and most of the Mar Menor resorts (to the Islas Pedrigueras, summer only). Sailing boats can be chartered for a privately tailored expedition. If you want to take a more detailed look at the local marine life without getting wet, hop aboard one of Benidorm's **glass-bottomed boats** *(see also ferries, page 92)*.

Boats tour the **Río Safari Elche** (tel: 965 638 288) outside Santa Pola. There are two local **safari parks**: **Vergel** (tel: 966 439 808, open every day of the year) near Pego, and **Aitana**, close to Relleu. This is the biggest wildlife park in Europe. You can also see animals at **Fort West**, a Wild West theme park near Campello, and at **La Nucia**'s small cowboy town and zoo. Benidorm's **Mundomar Marine and Exotic Animal Park** (daily all year, 9am–6pm) features what it claims is Europe's biggest dolphinarium, with dolphin and sea-lion shows.

For children's fairgrounds, **Festilandia** in Benidorm and **Festival Park** in Calpe are good, but they are rarely open in winter. Kids will probably enjoy Guadalest's museums of miniatures, **Mundo de Max** and **1,001 Curiosities**.

Go-karting is available at many places along the coast. For fun on smaller wheels, go **roller-skating** (rinks at Xàbia, Calpe, Benidorm and Alicante).

If rain or cold send you indoors, try Alicante's **Museo de Belenes** (Museum of Nativity Scenes; C. San Agustín 3 *(see page 37* for times). In **Villajoyosa** the **Museo de Chocolate** (tel: 965 890 950) is in Avda Gonzalo Sonano 13, Mon–Fri, Sat).

Watersports and Fishing

The warm calm Mediterranean is a paradise for watersports enthusiasts. The Mar Menor, immediately south of the Costa Blanca, is particularly noteworthy. If you don't have your own equipment, hire it on the beach or from a nautical club.

Windsurfers and small **sailing** dinghies may be hired on many beaches, but La Manga is best for the serious windsurfer or sailor. Calpe is the only place for **parasailing**. If the wind drops, hire a **speedboat** at Benidorm or **jet skis** at Dénia or Xàbia (Jávea) and let an engine do the work.

Water-skiing, available at many resorts, is an expensive sport to try. Check beforehand the length of the run, the permitted number of falls, and possible discounts for multiple runs. A cheaper alternative is **cable skiing** off the Playa de Levante in Benidorm.

You could also move under your own steam in a **pedal boat**, or try canoeing inland at Beniarrés dam.

The Amadorio dam (near Villajoyosa) and Guadalest dam are good places for **freshwater fishing**. You will need to obtain a licence from the appropriate government department, the *Consellería d'Agricultura i Pesca*, C. Professor Manel Sala 2, Alicante (tel: 96 593 4000). Ask for details in a tourist information office or fishing-tackle shop. Local fish include *barbel* (carp), bass and rainbow trout.

Under the Water

Snorkelling and **sub-aqua** are excellent in certain areas that have protected the submarine flora and fauna that thrives on the sea grass (*Posidonia oceanica*). Popular haunts include the Playa de Barraca (southeast of Xàbia), the Peñón de Ifach (Calpe), Playa de Torres (just east of Villajoyosa), Cabo de las Huertas (San Juan), the Cabo de Palos (La Manga) the islands of Benidorm and Hormigas – both now registered as marine reserves – and Tabarca, which still has the odd turtle swimming offshore.

For **sub-aqua**, a diving centre can usually provide a diving permit, equipment, a boat, tuition and tips about the local area. Alicante has more than 30 diving schools and the Mar Menor 12.

For contacts ring the Valencian Federació d'Activitats Subaquàtiques (tel: 963 154 491 or www.buceo-federado.com).

Snorkellers who swim away from the shore must tow a marker buoy for safety reasons. Watch out for sea urchins, wear flippers or plastic shoes when snorkelling or swimming near cliffs and rocks, and be careful where you put you hands.

If your accommodation does not have a swimming pool, cities and inland towns have a public outdoor pool, and most large towns have an indoor one.

On Land

There are **caves** with interesting stalactites and stalagmites at Benidoleig (Ondara),

Canalobre (Buslot) and Vall d'Ebo. Experienced riders can go **horse riding** in the mountains. For details of all these, ask in the local tourist offices.

Cycling has become popular: again, the tourist information offices can supply information on hiring bikes and routes, which are graded by difficulty.

Golf courses are numerous. Courses are open to visitors on payment of green fees and most clubs hire out equipment. The new 18-hole course at Playa San Juan, Alicante was designed by Severiano Ballesteros; there are another 18 courses in the province. El Club de la Manga is the most famous Murcian course. For all golf details, tel: 965 846 213 or 846 381.

Tennis is also very big in this area of Spain. Hotels with courts will often let non-residents play for a fee. At Villajoyosa, Eurotennis (tel: 96 589 1250) is a three-star hotel/apartment complex specialising in tennis holidays. Many towns have tennis clubs open to non-members.

Walking, Climbing and Nature Reserves

Various mountain ranges, nature reserves and sierras offer **walking and mountaineering** to heights of 1,500m (4,875ft). Major natural parks include the **Sierra de Espuña**, **Font Roja** and the **Sierra de Manola**.

A system of numbered Pequeños Recorridos (PRs), none of which are longer than 50 km (31 miles), are well signposted throughout the Alicante countryside. They range from walks through the Sierra Helada above Benidorm to coastal rambles from Santa Pola. For further further information, tel: 963 896 000.

The **Walkers' Train** (Trenet Senderista, tel: 965 878 515, 9–11pm) offers guided walks along the Dénia to Alicante route on Wednesdays and on weekends. Other interesting areas to explore are the Barrancos del Infierno and Mascarat, the Sierras d'Aitana, and de Mariola in the northern hill ranges, the Guardamar Dunes and small Murcian sierras (Yecla, Jumilla, de la Muela and Villafuerte) further south. The Cueva del Puero (tel: 968 745 162) has 11km (6½ miles) of tunnels, galleries and caves.

Left: the region attracts growing numbers of walkers

BEST BEACHES

This is a brief, selective guide to help choose a beach *(playa* or *platja)*, either for a quick visit in combination with one of the itineraries or for a long, lazy day's sunbathing and swimming. It includes Costa Cálida and Costa Blanca beaches.

The Costa Blanca falls into two halves: the northern bays and coves from Dénia to Alicante (divided by rocky headlands and backed by mountains), and the flat shoreline stretching south from Alicante to the regional border with Murcia and the Mar Menor.

There are some unspoilt beaches in the north: the rocky inlets of **Les Rotes** south of Dénia; the **Mar Azul** opposite **Portitxol**, the **Playa de Granadellas** and **Cala de los Tiestos** on the Cabo de la Nao; the coves north of Calpe, such as **Fustera** and **Pinets**, pebbly **L'Albir** and **Olla de Altea**, north of Benidorm, **Cala Tío Ximo** (Benidorm), and the bays south of Villajoyosa, such as **Cala del Xarco**. Many can be reached by rail as well as by road.

In Alicante, **Postiguet**, the city-centre beach, has a more local feel than **San Juan** or **La Albufereta**; the badly signposted **Cabo de la Huerta** has defied development and is good for snorkelling off the rocks.

South of Alicante, beaches are emptier and the development less continuous, but the high-rise resorts and villa estates stand out more brutally against the flat landscape. **Los Arenales**, within close range of Elche, has ugly apartment blocks, but a good stretch of gently sloping sand for children. **Tabarca**, Santa Pola's island, is inundated in summer because of the cool breezes on its small beach the island's coves have some of the most interesting sub-marine life on the coast.

Of the other beaches between here and the Mar Menor, **La Marina**, backed by pine forest, is good for shade, and **El Carabassí** just north of Santa Pola is protected from development. **Dehesa de Campoamor** (a 20-minute drive from Orihuela) has kept some unspoilt coves below rocky cliffs.

San Pedro del Pinatar, the first main Murcian resort, marks a shift to the warm, calm shallows, greyish sand and largely Spanish family tourism of the inland Mar Menor resorts. They are quietest between Los Alcázares and Los Nietos, where you can look over to the long sandy spit of **La Manga**, which is filled by traffic in summer. **Las Matas Gordas** is a narrow spit where the Mar Menor almost meets the Mediterranean. The finest beaches are around the corner. Known collectively as **Calblanque**, they have glassy-clear water, skin-diving and a rare wide horizon of undeveloped coast protected as *parque natural*.

South of Cartagena, **Calnegre** and **Cabo Cope**, which have been protected from development since 1994, are wild stretches of coast with small coves. **Bolnuevo** and **Azohía** are friendlier sandy beaches.

Nude Sunbathing

Topless sunbathing on the main beaches of the Costa Blanca and Costa Calida, is normal, and unlikely to offend locals. Nude sun-

bathing is permitted on: **Ambolo** (Cabo de la Nao), **Los Judíos** (Cabo de Huertas), **El Saladar** (south of Alicante city), **El Carabassí** (Elche district), **Los Tósales San Juan** (Guardamar), **Calblanque** (Murcia), and **La Marina** in **Portús** (just south of Cartagena).

Blue Flags

Costa Blanca and Costa Calida beaches have a good record – a total of 45 have been awarded EU 'Blue Flag' standards for cleanliness, safety and amenities – more than any other coast. Busy beaches have lifeguards, Red Cross posts and sometimes rescue boats. A green flag means the water is safe, a yellow flag means swimmers should be careful and a red flag means sea conditions are dangerous.

Above: the Playa del Postiguet, Alicante's city-centre beach, has a local feel

CALENDAR OF FIESTAS

Fiestas (*festas* in *Valenciano*) fuse historic traditions with regional customs. This brief calendar has a bias towards traditional popular culture and fiestas that are hospitable to outsiders, but there are literally hundreds of others. The dates of many move with the religious calendar. Get details from tourist offices or town halls.

5–6 January

Los Reyes Magos: Epiphany eve sees parades celebrating the arrival of the Three Kings. In Aledo and Cañada (near Villena), there are *autos*, or religious plays, on 6 Jan.

17–19 January

San Antón: The blessing of animals, horse-and-cart parades, with street bonfires.

Mid-February–Lent

Carnaval: Carnival, originally a pre-Lent feast, has returned in a wild, secular way in the past 20 years, with costumes – a lot of them transsexual – dancing through the night, big street parades and lots of drink.

Holy Week

Semana Santa: The processions all over Spain between Palm Sunday and Good Friday have interesting fervent rituals. Those in Murcia region are known for their processional images and baroque pageantry.

Particularly noteworthy (with days of the major processions indicated where relevant) are: Callosa de Segura (Wed and passion play on Good Friday); Cartagena (Wed, Fri, Sun); Crevillente; Elche (Palm Sunday procession in the town where all the Easter palms come from); Jumilla (Tues, Sun); Lorca (procession famed for the rivalry of the two brotherhoods, Azul and Blanco, on Good Friday); Mula and Moratalla (with *tamborada* drumming Wed, Thurs, Fri); Murcia city (Los Coloraos, Wed; Silencio, Thurs; Los Salzillos, Fri); Orihuela.

April

Fiestas de Perimavera (Spring festivals in Murcia city and the surrounding villages). A cross between a huge horticultural show and a general fiesta. The most traditional elements are the *Bando de la Huerta* – dancing, singing and satirical flower-laden floats – and the *Entierro de la Sardina* (literally 'Burial of the Sardine'), marking the end of Lent.

Pentecost Sunday

Festa del Xop (Planes): This is the oldest fiesta of Alicante province which guarantees fertility; a poplar tree is uprooted and planted in the main plaza and then scaled by the village's bachelors.

April–September

Moros y Cristianos (Alcoi, April 22–24; Caravaca, early May; Jijona, late Aug;

Above: effigies are burnt on St John's Night during Hogueras de San Juan in Alicante city

Lorca, Sept; Orihuela, late July; Villajoyosa, end of July; Villena, early Sept). Centuries-old and typically *alicantino*, these fiestas commemorate the Christian reconquest with parades of elaborately costumed Muslims and Christians and mock battles – leading to a Christian victory of course. Lots of bangs, gunpowder, fireworks and arcane rituals along the way. Alcoi's fiestas, on St George's Day, are the best known. At Caravaca de la Cruz, the *Caballos de Vino* is a horse race based on the famous occasion when the Knights Templar broke the Muslim siege to fetch drinking water.

May or June

Corpus Christi: Religious processions.

Late June

Hogueras de San Juan (Alicante city): The most famous and popular of the city's fiestas, with effigies burnt on St John's Night after a week of all-night street parties and live music. The fiesta dates from the 1920s, but the tradition of fire festivals on summer solstice is pre-Christian. Midnight fireworks over the bay follow the *Nit del Foc*. Smaller *Hogueras* take place around the same time in Jávea, Dénia, Benidorm, Calpe and Pego.

July

Santísima Sangre (Dénia): 1st weekend July. These annual fiestas include a battle of flowers and the *bous en la mar*, in which bulls are released on the quayside – either they or their human persecutors fall into the sea.
Fiesta del Carmen (Tarbarca, San Pedro del Pinatar and other Mar Menor villages, Villajoyosa): The main fiesta of Spanish fishing ports. Images of the *Virgen del Carmen*, the fishermen's saint, are carried round the harbour and/or taken out to sea to bless the decked-out fleet.

Mid-August

Castell de l'Olla (Olla de Altea): Spectacular late-night firework display over the sea on the Sat closest to 10 Aug.

Fiestas de la Vendimia (Jumilla): a week-long fiesta celebrating the grape harvest. The town fountain runs with wine.
Xocolatissima! La Vila Joisa's chocolate

festival with a walking route, tastings, cookery courses etc.

September

Fiestas de Cartagineses y Romanos (Cartagena): similar to the *Moros y Cristianos* but this fiesta celebrates the expulsion of the Romans from the city.

ARTS & CULTURAL FESTIVALS

Early August

Festival Nacional del Cante de las Minas (La Unión): Flamenco mining songs were introduced by immigrant Andalucian mine workers and a competition and festival helps keep them going today. Held every year in the modernist market building. Tickets are available from tourist offices; Cajamurcia from July. Info: www.cantedelasminas.org

Mid-August

Certamen Internacional de Habaneras y Polifonía (Torrevieja): the rhythmic choral *habaneras* were brought to Spain by 19th-century sailors and exporters from Cuba. A week-long programme. For tickets tel: 96 571 2570.

Early September

Festival de Folklore del Mediterráneo (Murcia): This festival highlights a different country each year, but there are always participating groups from all over the world.

Right: re-enacting the Reconquest

Practical Information

GETTING THERE

By Air
Both British Airways and Iberia operate scheduled flights to the Costa Blanca. If you can be flexible about your departure date and time, you should be able to pick up a cheaper charter deal to Alicante. A number of companies such as Easyjet and Spainair operate cut price flights.

The area has two airports: El Altet (tel: 96 691 9000), 10km (6 miles) to the southwest of Alicante, and San Javier (tel: 968 172 000), on the coast 40km (25 miles) to the southeast of Murcia.

Transport to and from Airports
Some international car-hire firms have branches at the airports where you can collect or hire a car.

A taxi ride from **El Altet airport** (€12) to the centre of Alicante takes 15 minutes. Buses run to and from town every 20 minutes between 6.55am and 11.15pm; the journey time is roughly 20 minutes.

A bus runs between Valencia bus station and **Manises airport** at hourly intervals between about 6am and 9pm. Allow 45 minutes for the trip.

From **San Javier airport**, you will need to get a taxi to La Ribera (3km), then a bus to Murcia. The bus leaves once every two hours and the journey takes one hour.

By Boat
There are two direct car ferry routes from Britain to Spain. Brittany Ferries sails from Plymouth to Santander (tel: 08703 665333;) and P&O European ferries from Portsmouth to Bilbao (tel: 08705 202020). Both crossings take over 24 hours. Rough seas can cause cancellations in autumn and winter.

By Car
To drive from Britain to southeastern Spain will take at least two or three days or 30 hours minimum if you drive non-stop, even if you travel on the French toll motorways. Allow 10–15 hours for the road journey from Santander to Alicante.

Your car must be equipped with a wing mirror on each side, headlamp deflectors, two warning triangles and a set of spare light bulbs. For peace of mind, consider taking out continental cover with a reputable breakdown service such as RACE (tel: 96 522 9349 and 968 250 122)

You will need a 'green card' (international insurance certificate), your registration document and a Spanish bail bond. This document will prevent the Spanish police from locking you up if you injure somebody in an accident. It is advisable to carry an International Driving Permit or a Spanish translation of your driving licence; some kind of licence must be carried at *all* times.

By Coach
Coach travel to the Costa Blanca is relatively cheap, but the journey – from London via the Channel ports and France, then down the Spanish coast past Valencia and on to Alicante and Murcia – takes an arduous 1½ days, so be warned and take a good book.

By Train
Tickets for journeys between the UK and Spain can be obtained from any leading travel agents in the UK or from Rail Europe, tel: 08705 848 848, www.raileurope.co.uk (from the US, tel: 1-877-257 2887; www.raileurope.com). Thomas Cook publishes a comprehensive European timetable, which is available from its branch offices.

Left: Alicante port
Above: ceramic street sign in Xàbia

TRAVEL ESSENTIALS

When to Go

The Costa Blanca, protected by mountain ranges, enjoys a mild Mediterranean climate with year-round sunshine, low rainfall and moderately high humidity. July and August are often hot, with temperatures reaching 35°C (95°F). The coolest months of the year are January and February, when temperatures range from a low 7°C (44°F) to a pleasant 17°C (63°F). These also tend to be the wettest months of the year, along with March and April.

Thick, heavy clothes are unnecessary, even in winter. Sunglasses are essential if you are doing a lot of driving.

During the summer months many banks, department stores, high-class hotels, restaurants and public transport vehicles are air-conditioned. In winter some hotels and restaurants, particularly in the higher, cooler regions, are centrally heated.

The sea temperature is ideal for bathing from April to early November, although braver swimmers can be spotted taking a dip in winter.

February and March are the best months to see and smell the pink-and-white almond blossom. During the spring months lemon and orange blossoms, and many other Mediterranean plants are in flower. If you are a birdwatcher, go in winter to see the spectacle of migrating flamingos at the saltpans and lakes along the coast south of Alicante.

Entry Requirements

British and other EU nationals, as well as nationals from the US, Australia and New Zealand need only a valid passport to enter Spain for a period of up to three months. Visitors from other countries should check with their nearest Spanish embassy.

What to Wear

Spanish people tend to dress with a casual elegance, but it is perfectly acceptable to wear scruffy or beach clothes in tourist areas. You should be well covered when visiting churches, monasteries, etc. Nor is it a good idea to explore inland areas in skimpy beach wear.

Electricity

Plugs have two round pins. Voltage is 220 AC. A converter and/or an adaptor plug may be useful if you want to take electrical appliances with you.

Time

Spain is one hour ahead of Greenwich Mean Time (GMT). In January, the sun rises at about 8.15am and sets at about 6pm; the corresponding times in June are 5.45am and 8.15pm, although the light lingers for another two hours.

GETTING ACQUAINTED

Crowds

July and August are the peak months for tourists, both Spanish and foreign. This is a good time if you like lively coastal resorts. However, if you are looking for a peaceful holiday and want to avoid inflated prices and traffic jams, especially at the beginning and end of August and for the holiday weekend (14–15 August), you are advised to stay away from the coast during this period.

Fiestas

At all times of year you are sure to find a fiesta or an arts festival somewhere *(see Calendar of Fiestas)*. If you value your sleep, make your base outside the town and travel

Above: freshly baked in Benissa

in for the festivities (but remember that roads in the centre are often closed to non-residents). Sightseeing can be frustrating at fiesta time: it is hard to make your way around, and shops and museums may be closed.

Please note, too, that fiesta and festival tickets are usually available only direct from *ayuntamientos*.

Language

English is spoken by many people, as you would expect in a major tourist area. However, you will probably find a phrase book useful, and it is worth learning at least a few basic expressions before you go. A small effort on your part will help you to make friends with local people.

Attitudes to Tourists

British tourists do not have a very good reputation on the Costa Blanca as a result of the behaviour of *los hooligans*. However, the Spanish emphasise that the offenders are not only British, and locals often tend to be surprisingly friendly.

Attitudes to Children

The Spanish dote on children, and they are sure to be given a warm welcome wherever they go; hotels are very understanding about their needs and will do their best to provide meals to suit.

You are unlikely to find a babysitter except by means of an informal personal arrangement, but it is part of the Spanish way of life for children to accompany adults to cafés, restaurants and fiestas, even very late at night.

Religion

Roman Catholicism is dominant throughout Spain, but only Anglican and Evangelical churches have Christian services in English (see local English-language press for details). There is a scattering of Jehovah's Witness churches throughout the area, as well as a synagogue in Benidorm and Buddhist temple in Benimantell.

Visiting churches can be tricky because, unless they are major landmarks, they are generally open only at the times of Mass, i.e. early morning and early evening, and all Sunday morning. At other times, or for smaller churches, you usually need to ask for the priest *(cura)*, who may be available to give you the key and/or show you around. Monasteries and convents are open all day; ring the doorbell to be admitted.

Sex

There is a large divide in Spanish attitudes to sex: part of the population has become liberal since Franco's death, as a cursory glance at Spanish TV will confirm, while others remain dogmatically conservative. Legally, the minimum age for sex, both heterosexual and homosexual, between two consenting people is 15. All contraceptives are available at chemists, and condoms can be bought at supermarkets.

Harassment

Some women experience unwanted attention from local men. Historically, the Spanish have perceived foreign women as more likely than Spanish ones to be available for sex. On the whole, it is quite safe to travel alone, but if you are on the nervous side you may want to consider taking a personal alarm with you.

MONEY MATTERS

The Euro (€) is Spain's official currency, officially replacing the peseta in 2002 at a fixed exchange rate of 1 Euro to 166.4 pesetas. Coins are produced to the value of 1, 2, 5, 10, 20, 50 cents, and 1 and 2 Euro. Notes are available in 5, 10, 20, 50, 100, 200, 500 Euro denominations.

Getting Cash

There are no restrictions on the movement of capital within the Euro countries. Exchange rates for non-Euro currencies are generally similar for cash as for travellers' cheques, and banks usually give you the best deal, generally 0.2 percent. If you change large sums of money at one time, you'll probably save on commission, but you'll have more to lose if you're mugged; and of course you could have more to change back at the end of your stay.

Travellers' cheques (available in Euros)

Natural History

Since the 1970s, the areas of Spanish coast and countryside protected or marked out for the value of their landscape and wildlife have increased enormously, highlighting their importance and value, previously overlooked. There are various classifications: *parque natural* and *parque natural terrestre-marítimo* (the latter covering both sea and shore), which are the most stringently protected; *paraje natural*, an interesting landscape; *reserva de caza* and *reserva integral*, protecting the wildlife. These are marked on maps, although sometimes not very accurately, since some proposals for protection haven't come to fruition due to opposition from local landowners and/or industry, and others are too recent to be included on maps.

Along the coast itself, some capes and offshore islands have kept a remarkable submarine life, which flourishes on the sea grass (*Posidonia oceanica*). It used to cover the entire continental platform, but is now only left in patches. For this reason Tabarca, where it is still possible to see turtles, is a marine reserve with controlled public access. Other areas that stand out are the Islote de Benidorm and the Islas Hormigas (both marine reserves), the Cap de la Nao, and Calblanque, protected as *espacios naturales*.

The larger *parques naturales* within the Costa Blanca region are the pine forests of the Sierra de Espuña (the second largest *parque* in Spain), the Carrascal de Font Roja, which is an important last outpost of mixed Mediterranean woodland with *carrascas* (kermes oaks), and the Serra de Mariola, both close to Alcoi. But there are others within Alicante province, such as the Peñón d'Ifach, which has interesting plant life and Pico del Montgó to the south of Dénia.

The string of salt lakes down the coast were upgraded from *parajes naturales* to *parques naturales* in 1994 and are host to much interesting bird life, including flamingoes, grebes, numerous species of wading birds including avocets, black-winged stilts and other migratory species which are particularly numerous during the spring and autumn migrations. The Lagunas de la Mata and Torrevieja, and the inland Laguna del Hondo have all been transformed in recent years into important protected areas of rare bird life. Some 250 recorded species have been observed at the Salinas de Santa Pola.

Besides this, there are areas of great beauty and interest with no special protection: the Barrancos del Infierno and Mascarat, the Sierra d'Aitana, the Guardamar Dunes and small Murcian sierras (for example Yecla, Jumilla, de la Muela and Villafuerte). As elsewhere in Spain, the rural areas are rich in birdlife – with colourful bee-eaters, rollers and hoopoes, larger birds such as storks and herons, and raptors including various species of buzzards, eagles and, in the mountains, Egyptian and Black vultures.

Last but not least, there are the exotic *palmerales,* or palm forests, thought to have been planted by the Phoenicians. Among these Elche's municipal park and the privately owned Hort del Cura are outstanding.

In all these areas you can follow a series of signed and marked paths. Most have an information centre where you can pick up details of routes and more information about the wildlife. Alicante provinces Pequeños Recorridos (PRs) are particularly well organised in this regard.

Left: barn owls are one of several species of owl found in the region

are the safest way to bring your money. They cannot, however, be used to pay for goods directly. Remember to make a note of the serial numbers and to keep this separate from the cheques.

Having money sent to Spain from abroad is complicated, expensive and time-consuming, and should be done in emergencies only. Contact your bank for further details.

Credit Cards

Many hotels, up-market restaurants and all department stores take credit cards, Visa and MasterCard being the most widely accepted. Most credit cards can be used to obtain cash. You can withdraw money over the counter during banking hours; if you know your Personal Identification Numbers (PIN), you will also have access to cash from 24-hour dispensers, usually with a modest handling fee charged by your bank. If you use a credit card the exchange rate will be the one that is current when your cash advance is processed. Numbers for lost or stolen credit cards are as follows: Visa and Mastercard 91 519 2100, Amex 91 572 0303, Diners 91 547 4000.

GETTING AROUND

By Car

Remember to drive on the right and overtake on the left. This may sound elementary, but it is easy to forget on empty country roads.

Seat belts are compulsory. Speed limits are 60kph (38mph) in built-up areas, 100kph (62mph) on major roads, and 120kph (75mph) on motorways. Speeding fines are high and are payable on the spot. Children under 13 must sit in the back seat. Spanish law states that you must carry a spare set of headlamp bulbs and a warning triangle.

In large town or city centres, on-street parking spaces are hard to find, although expensive multi-storey car parks generally have room. Anarchic and double parking are national pastimes in Spain, but don't be fooled into thinking that the police never give parking tickets or tow cars away.

Petrol grades are super (97 octane), normal (92 octane), unleaded (95 octane) and diesel. Unleaded petrol is available everywhere.

There are two kinds of motorway in Spain: *autopista* (which you must pay a toll to use) and *autovía* (which is free). An expensive toll is levied on the coastal motorway north of Alicante (about €5 Alicante to Dénia, for example). There are no charges south of Alicante except on the new Ausur toll motorway from Crevillente to Cartagena (A37). This is due to be extended to Sax. The motorways are a good investment in summer and during the rest of the year in rush hours, which are linked to exoduses from towns at weekends and holidays, and influxes to town for highjinks at night and the return to work at the end of the weekends. The lunch and siesta period (approximately 2–5pm) is a good time to travel. Local roads to beaches are often congested on public holidays and Sundays in summer. The new inland motorway from Valencia to Murcia via Alcoy and Sax is due for completion in 2006.

Maps are not always up-to-date and there are constant major roadworks: currently, for example, Alicante city's new ring road; the Via Parque linking the N332 to the Playa de San Juan, and, inland, stretches of the N-340. In case of an accident, there are SOS points every 5km (3 miles) on major roads; the police emergency phone number is 091. Make sure you obtain full details from any other driver involved. Any injury, however slight, has to be reported to the police, and the injured person must be taken to hospital.

Hiring a Car

A British travel agent should be able to arrange car hire for you, but small local companies are generally cheaper than big international ones. If you're under 23 and/or you have less than two years' driving experience, you'll find it difficult to rent a car.

You will need your passport and an International Driving Permit (your British licence will probably be accepted). All firms charge a set fee per day, plus IVA (tax) and insurance. Some firms charge extra for mileage. A deposit is required unless you pay by credit card with monthly billing.

Hiring a Moped or Bicycle

Bicycles and mopeds for hire are easy to find in coastal resorts, and relatively cheap.

To hire a moped, you must be aged 16 or over and have your passport and driving licence. Helmets are compulsory. Mopeds use *mezcla* (mixed) petrol.

By Taxi

Taxis are good for getting around towns and are generally cheaper than in Britain. An available taxi displays either a green light or a sign saying *libre*. The meter should be running. Surcharges are added to the basic fare at night (11pm to 6am), at weekends and on public holidays, for trips outside the city and to the airport, and for luggage. Tipping (5–10 percent of the fare) is expected.

By Coach

There is no single national coach line; ask at tourist offices where you need to go for your destination. Local coach services can only be booked and paid for in Spain, and reservations should be made. Coach stations are organised according to the company, not the route. Alicante station, tel: 965 130 700, Murcia station, tel: 968 292 211.

By Train and Tram

Tickets can be bought at train stations, RENFE (the Spanish railway network) travel offices or any authorised travel agency at any time between 60 days and 5 minutes before departure. There are different types of train, varying in price and speed from the fast *talgo* down to the slow *exprés*.

Discount fares are available on off-peak days *(días azules)*. On production of suitable identification, senior citizens, families with children and young people under 26 can also obtain discounts. You can buy a tourist pass valid for unlimited travel within Spain for periods of 8, 15 or 22 days. The relevant mainline routes within this area are Cartagena–Alicante–Valencia, Alicante–Madrid and Cartagena–Murcia–Albacete–Madrid. The fast Euromed service to Valencia from Alicante takes 1½ hours; Alicante to Madrid takes 4 hours. A high-speed line from Madrid to Valencia, Alicante and Murcia is due to open in 2006. Information and reservations, tel: 902 24 02 02.

The FGV tram and narrow-gauge train *(see page 27)* leaves Alicante from the station next to Postiguet beach every 30 minutes. At Campello you switch to a train.

The Lemon Express, an early 20th-century wooden train, uses the same line, and runs from Benidorm to Gata and back from Tues–Sat. Reservations can be made at Benidorm station, tel: 96 680 3103. Walkers' trains run at weekends from Sept–May, tel: 965 878 515 (9–11pm).

By Sea

You can find out about or book the following ferry services through any local travel agency.

Hydrofoil and boat to Ibiza: Balearia, tel: 902 160 180, runs daily hydrofoil and boat services from Dénia to Ibiza and Palma.

Ferries to the Balearics: Trasmediterranea, tel: 902 454 645, has regular sailings from the port of Valencia to Mallorca, Menorca and Ibiza.

Ferry to Tabarca: The shortest journey is via Santa Pola (25 minutes); this route and the one from Alicante are both operated by Kontiki, tel: 96 521 6396, running from April to November, the frequency varying according to the season and weather. The

longest route, between Torrevieja and Tabarca, takes one and half hours and runs daily June to September.

HOURS AND HOLIDAYS

Business Hours

Most shops open from 9am–1pm and 4–8pm Mon–Sat; in resort towns many stay open on Sundays. Department stores and some high street chains do not close for lunch.

Post offices are open from 9am–2pm Monday–Friday, and from 9am–1pm on Saturday.

Banks operate Mon–Fri from 8.30am or 9am to 2 pm; some branches stay open on Saturday, but close an hour earlier. Outside banking hours, you may be able to change money at a hotel, station, airport or department store.

Public Holidays

The following dates are public holidays in both Alicante province and Murcia region: 1 and 6 January, 19 March, Easter Thursday, Good Friday, 1 May, 15 August, 12 October, 1 November, 6, 8 and 25 December; 9 June is also a public holiday in Murcia; 19 March and 9 October in Alicante. Local holidays are in late April (Murcia spring festivals) June (San Juan), on the Monday of Easter week and on Thursday after Easter (Santa Faz).

If you are planning to travel to the Costa Blanca over the Christmas or Easter periods, do not worry about finding everything shut down for weeks – this is not the case.

WHERE TO STAY

Hotels

Hotels are graded from one to five stars, *hostales* from one to three and *pensiones* from one to two. The appropriate category is displayed on a blue plaque at the entrance. If you are looking for atmosphere, you can't beat the state-run chain of *paradores*. These luxury hotels are often in renovated convents or castles or, like the one in Xàbia (Jávea), modern buildings in privileged settings. At the other end of the market there are

increasing numbers of bed and breakfasts and country houses to rent *(casas rurales)* appearing away from the coast.

All hotels are required to display prices (including service and tax) at the reception desk and in every bedroom, and to have a complaints book *(Hoja Oficial de Reclamaciones)* for customers' use. Any complaint must be sent to the relevant authorities within 48 hours, so a request to use the book will probably solve any argument.

The following list is a selection of hotels that have character, are in pleasant locations and are a little different from the run-of-the-mill establishments. They are all popular so its best to book ahead. The hotels have been rated as follows (prices relate to a double room with bathroom, during high season):

$ = under €45
$$ = €45–90
$$$ = over €90

In Towns
Alicante/Alacant

Mediterranean Plaza (four stars)
Pl. del Ayuntamiento 6
Tel: 965 210 188
Email: info@hotelmediterraneanplaza.com
Sleek 50-room hotel in the old town with gym and sauna, close to the beach. $$$.

Pension Les Monges Palace (two stars)
C. Monjas 2–10
Tel: 965 215 046
www.lesmonges.net
Modernism and Mediterranean styles meet in this great pension in the old town; garage, computer lines and TV. No restaurant. $–$$.

Altea

Hostal Fornet (one star)
C. Beniardá 1
Tel: 96 584 3005
Some rooms have a terrace and sea views. Garage for supplement. $$.

Cartagena

Los Habaneros (two stars)
San Diego 60
Tel: 968 505 250
Email: hotelhabaneros@fotodigital.es
Friendly 1950s hotel, very well positioned for exploring the old town and harbour. $$.

Left: most shops are open until 8pm, but close for lunch

La Manga del Mar Menor
Hyatt Regency la Manga
Los Belones
Tel: 968 331 234
Email: hrlaman@hyatt-intl.com
Part of the luxurious complex La Manga Club, built in the style of a Spanish village. Facilities include golf courses, swimming pools, tennis courts and a health centre. $$$

Dénia
MR Hotels Les Rotes (two stars)
Partida Las Rotas 71
Tel: 96 578 0323
By the sea just outside Dénia. Refurbished old hotel with tennis court, and restaurant leading out to pool (Apr–Oct). Parking. $$–$$$

Elche/Elx
Huerto del Cura (four stars)
Porta de la Morera 14
Tel: 96 661 0011
Email: comercial@huerta-delcura.com
Modern *parador* in the palm forest, including individual chalets in an attractive garden. Swimming pool and tennis court. Covered parking. $$$

Lorca
Alameda (three stars)
Tel: 968 406 600
Email: info@hotel-alameda.com
Pleasant small hotel in the Alameda gardens. No restaurant. Parking. Prices double in Holy Week. $$

Murcia
Hotel Arco de San Juan (four stars)
Pl. de Ceballos 10
Tel: 968 210 455
Email: info@arcosanjuan.com
Built on the site of an 18th-century palace and retaining the original façade. Unusual décor and many works of art; parking. $$$.

Torrevieja
Hotel Madrid (two stars)
C. Villa Madrid 15
Tel: 96 571 1350
Email: hmadrid@murelo-free.com
Functional but comfortable hotel close to the motorway (Crevillente turnoff) and salt lagoons. $$.

Xàbia/Jávea
Parador de Jávea (four stars)
Avda Mediterranea 7
Tel: 96 579 0200
Email: javea@parador.es
Uninspiring architecture, but privileged position on the seafront with swimming pool and garden; garage. $$$.

Off the Beaten Track
Agres
Pensión Mariola (no stars)
C. San Antonio 4, on road into village
.Tel: 96 551 0017
Plain rooms, comfortable lounge and rustic dining room; parking. $.

Alfafara
Casa Rural El Pinet
Masía El Pinet s/n
Sierra Mariola
Tel: 96 552 9039
Founding member of rural tourism scheme; the 18th-century farmhouse has double and triple rooms, swimming pool, and a six-person flat. $$.

Balneario de Archena
Hotel Termas (four stars)
Carr. Balneario s/n
Tel: 968 670 100
Email: reservas@balneario-dearchena.com
Access via stairs and tunnels to baths and fountains below. Very elegant. Covered parking. Three swimming pools. $$–$$$.

Left: bougainvillaea adorns a typical village street

Baños de Mula
Baños el Poco
Tel: 968 661 397
Small family hotel with flats and spa baths. Can also be rented by the hour. Also: El Delfin (tel: 968 661 227) and Parador Azul (tel: 968 661 205).

Bullas
Hospedería Molino de Abajo
Ctra de Totana s/n
Tel: 968 431 383
Idyllic and very comfortable converted watermill with horse-riding, river swimming and an excellent restaurant. $$.

Confrides
Hotel El Pirineo (no stars)
C. San Antonio 52
Tel/fax: 96 588 5858
Good base for exploring Costa Blanca; inland but within easy reach of the coast. Homely family-run hotel, local cooking; parking. $

Moratalla
Hostal Levante (one star)
Carr. del Canal 21
Tel: 968 730 454
Outside the village centre. Family-run bar-restaurant with rooms upstairs. Parking. $.

Tabarca
Casa del Gobernador (2 stars)
C. Arzola s/n
Tel: 965 960 886
Email: cajadelgobernador@ctr.es
Wonderful island hotel inside a historic building, with local cooking. $$.

Renting a Villa

Self-catering accommodation is usually rented for at least a week, and usually in monthly or fortnightly blocks. Characterful local houses can be tracked down via the regional rural tourism schemes. Contact: www.murcia-turismo.com/rural.htm www.comunitat-valenciana.com, under Turismo Rural.

Camping and Caravanning

Most campsites are concentrated along the coast, and only the official sites are legal.

No Number
The presence of s/n in a Spanish address denotes *sin número*, which translates as "without number"; such unhelpfully un-numbered buildings are normally large – hospitals, schools and large hotels.

They are classified according to their fees and amenities: ranging from luxury, then first to third class. Most campsites have running water and electricity. Prices, which at the more luxurious sites are similar to those of a cheap hotel, must be displayed at the entrance of the site.

At many sites it is possible to camp all year round, although outside the peak summer months there may be fewer amenities and the site may have a slightly depressing out-of-season feel.

The following list contains a selection of well-run sites that are open throughout the year.

Benidorm: Caravanning-Camping Villasol (first class), Camino Viejo de Valencia s/n, tel: 96 585 0422; www.camping-villasol.com. Central and luxurious. Indoor and outdoor swimming pools.

Elche/Elx: Camping El Palmeral, C. Curtidores s/n, tel: 968 542 2766. In the middle of the palm forest. Swimming pool.

Camping Internacional la Manna, Ctra N332 km 76, tel: 965 419 051; www.camping-lamarina.com. 5-star site.

Moratalla: La Puerta (second class), tel: 968 730 008; www.campinglapuerta.com. Beautifully situated model campsite in forest in river valley with waterfall. Has a swimming pool, tennis court, barbecues, spring water. Nearby Bullas also has a good site. Also has houses to rent.

HEALTH & EMERGENCIES

If you are not used to strong sun you should take the usual precautions. In summer, sightseeing is best restricted to the early morning or late afternoon, when the heat is more bearable than it is in the middle of the day. The Spanish don't have a midday siesta for nothing!

practical information

Eating and Drinking

Not all tap water on the Costa Blanca is drinkable, and none of it has a particularly pleasant taste. Bottled mineral water, sparkling *(con gas)* or still *(sin gas)*, is readily available in shops and restaurants. Fruit and vegetables should always be washed carefully. If you are caught short, don't hesitate to use the toilets in a bar or petrol station; this is common practice because there aren't many public toilets elsewhere.

Chemists

A green or red cross sign identifies a chemist *(farmacia)*. They are generally open from 9.30am–2pm and from 4pm–8pm on weekdays, and for the morning hours only on Saturday. Outside these times, a list of on-duty chemists providing an emergency 24-hour service can be found on the door of each pharmacy.

Spanish pharmacists are highly trained paramedics, and can deal with many minor ailments. You can freely buy some medicines, including certain antibiotics, that in Britain are available only on prescription.

You can get a large discount on the cost of medicines if you have a Spanish doctor's prescription; you may find it difficult to use a foreign prescription in Spain but you may buy the product at full-price.

National Health Services

If you are an EU resident and have an E111 form (obtainable from the Dept. of Social Security) you are eligible for free treatment from the Spanish national health service. For extra protection, take out medical insurance as well. Vaccinations are not needed for visitors from Britain.

If your case is urgent, ask a chemist or your hotel for directions to the nearest public hospital *(residencia* or *hospital)*; take the original and a photocopy of your E111 form if you have one; if not, take your passport along instead.

Facilities for the Disabled

Although awareness of the needs of disabled people is increasing, facilities, such as lifts and adapted toilets are still few in number.

Crime & Emergencies

Take elementary precautions to avoid being the victim of crime. In coastal resorts and big towns, you should beware of pickpockets and bag snatchers. Make full use of hotel safes. Don't sit in your car with your bag or purse on your lap; it may be snatched by thieves on a motorbike. Don't leave valuables in your car and watch your possessions carefully if you are on the beach.

If anything is stolen, go to the local police

A Note on Language

Since 1982 Alicante province has been bilingual along with the rest of the autonomous region of Valencia. *Valenciano* – now on an equal legal footing with *castellano* (or Spanish) after years of suppression under Franco – is a written and spoken language closely related to Catalan. *Valenciano* has its own literature and is now the language of local government, as well as regional television and radio. Murcia uses only *castellano*, though sometimes with the dying local dialect of *panocho*.

On an everyday spoken basis, however, the reality is more complex than this. The northern third of Alicante province remains solidly *valenciano* speaking and another wedge in the south – around Elche and the Segura valley – is rapidly becoming so now

that young people are learning *valenciano* at school. However, *castellano* continues to dominate in Alicante city, the Vinalopo valley, Orihuela and other border areas with Murcia and, of course, in many of the coastal resorts. Road and street signs, maps, local newspapers and other printed information reflect this regional shading and are not yet consistently bilingual.

As a result, *Insight Pocket Guide: Costa Blanca* is not entirely consistent either. City and town listings give both *castellano* and *valenciano* placenames where they differ (for example, Elche and Elx) and names of museums and restaurants are given as they were found. In general references within the text, both are used as appropriate to the context, although *castellano* tends to occur more frequently than *valenciano*.

station; the police are unlikely to find your belongings, but you will need to fill in a form for insurance purposes.

While wandering around old quarters, you may be approached by drug dealers. Drug dealing and trafficking are illegal in Spain.

Useful numbers: police line to report minor crimes, tel: 902 102 112; fire brigade 085; ambulance 061; local police 092; national police 091; guardia civil 062; **British Consulate** in Alicante, tel: 96 521 6022); **British Consulate** in Benidorm, tel: 965 850 123; **Irish Consulate** in Alicante, tel: 965 107 485; **US Consulate** in Valencia, tel: 96 351 6973.

COMMUNICATIONS & MEDIA

Post

Stamps can be purchased at tobacconists *(estancos)* as well as at post offices. Airmail to Britain takes two to ten days to arrive – less if you pay an extra charge to send it *urgente*, and you put it in a red postbox (standard letters go in yellow ones).

Telephone, Fax and Internet

Public phone boxes have instructions for use in English. There are also large telephone offices where calls are paid for after they have been made; you can make a reverse-charge call *(cobro revertido)* from these offices or from a call box. Many bars, hotels, restaurants and petrol stations have coin-operated phones. For Spanish directory enquiries dial 11888 or 11818; for international enquiries dial 025. If you wish to bring your mobile phone, contact your network for details – arrangements and costs vary widely. It may be cheaper for you to rent a mobile in Spain.

To call other countries first dial the international access code 00, then the relevant country code. If you are using a US credit phone card, dial the company's access number below, then 01, and then the country code. Sprint tel: 900 99 0013; AT&T tel: 900 99 0011. The international code for Spain is 34; the area code for Alicante and Valencia provinces is 96 and for Murcia province 968. You need to use this area code at all times even if you are phoning within a province or indeed within a small town.

You are likely to be able to fax from a printer, copy shop or stationer *(papelería)*. Internet is available in certain large post offices and many cyber cafés along the coast and in large cities.

Newspapers

National newspapers you might find interesting include *El País* (centre-left), *Diario 16* and *ABC* (centre-right) and *El Mundo* (unclear). The *Costa Blanca News* and the *Entertainer* are published in English and are targeted primarily at expatriate residents, as is the glossy magazine *Lookout*. They are available mostly in coastal resorts, where the international press can also be bought a day after publication.

Events Listings

These can be found in all of the publications mentioned above. Town halls and tourist offices often publicise events. For information in advance of your visit, log on to www.lanetro.com, a listings website.

English-Language Books

Don't expect to find anything other than popular fiction paperbacks on sale. Most large bookshops sell at least some English-

language books: the best in Alicante is Ochenta Mundos (Marqués de Molins 65, tel: 965 200 439) and FNAL (Avda de la Estación 5). There are English-language bookshops dotted along the coast, at Alfaz del Pi, Benidorm, Calpe, Dénia, Xàbia (Jávea) and Torrevieja, where international newspapers are also available.

Above: directions to the post office

TV and Radio

There are two national public television channels in Spanish (Castilian): TVE1 and TVE2. There are also two private channels (Antenna 3 and Tele 5), and the subscription-only Canal +. International satellite channels, including English-language ones, are available in hotels and bars. The Alicante area also receives the regional television channel Canal 9, in Valencian, and TVE3, in Catalan. Murcia receives Canal Sur from Andalucia.

The BBC World Service can be picked up on a short-wave radio. Frequencies are 15.070MHz/19.19m and 12.095MHz/24.80m.

Some local radio stations have a small part of their output in English: you can check the local English-language press for details.

USEFUL ADDRESSES

Tourist Information Offices

Opening hours vary, and fluctuate considerably. Most offices are open for approximately four hours in the morning and another three hours in the late afternoon, Monday to Saturday, and Sunday mornings. During the summer months some are open longer, and large towns often set up temporary summer offices in addition to the all-year-round ones. Even if you are somewhere which doesn't have a tourist office, the town hall may be able to help.

General tourist information numbers are Alicante, tel: 902 100 910 and Murcia tel: 902 101 070. Websites are www.costablanca.org and www.murciaturistica.es

Alcoi/Alcoy: C. San Lorenzo 2, tel: 96 553 7155.

Alicante/Alacant: tel: 96 520 0000; C. Portugal 17, by the coach station, tel: 96 592 9802; Alicante Airport, tel: 96 691 9367.

Altea: C. St Pierre 9, tel: 96 584 4114.

Benidorm: Avda. Martínez Alejos 16, in the old town near the town hall, tel: 96 585 3224.

Calpe/Calp: Avda. Ejércitos Españoles 66, between the seafront and the old town, tel: 96 583 8532.

Caravaca de la Cruz: C. de las Monjas 17, tel: 968 702 424.

Cartagena: Pza Bastarreche s/n, tel: 968 521 427

Dénia: Plaza Oculista Buigues 9, tel: 96 642 2367.

Elche/Elx: Parque Municipal s/n, tel: 96 545 3831.

Gandía: C. Marqués de Campo s/n, in front of train station, tel: 96 284 2407.

La Manga: Los Amoladeras, tel: 968 146 136.

Lorca: Palacio Guerara C. Lopez Gisbert s/n, tel: 968 466 157.

Los Alcázares: Avda Trece de Octubre 13, tel: 968 171 361.

Mula: Convento San Francisco, C. Doña Elvira, tel: 968 661 501.

Murcia: C. San Cristóbal 6, tel: 968 358 749.

Orihuela/Oriola: C. Francisco Díez 25, near the town hall, tel: 96 530 2747.

Santa Pola: Pl. de la Diputacíon 6, tel: 96 699 2276.

Torrevieja: Plaza Ruíz Capdepont s/n, tel: 96 570 3433.

Xàbia/Jávea: Pl. del Almirante Bastarreche 24, by the port, tel: 96 579 0736.

Xàtiva/Játiva: Alameda Jaime I 50, tel: 96 227 3346.

In England: 22–23 Manchester Square, London W1M 5AP, tel: 020 7486 8077 (Mon–Fri 9.15am–4.15pm) or 0900 166 9920 (24-hour brochure request line). You can also visit the tourist office's informative website: www.tourspain.es

FURTHER READING

There are very few books dealing with this region in isolation. For more information, log onto the **Instituto Cervantes** website (www.fourlanguages.org).

Insight Guide: Spain. Apa Publications, 2003. Comprehensive coverage of sights and attractions, superb photographs, full-colour maps and detailed practical information.

The Face of Spain, Gerald Brenan. Penguin, 1988 (first published in 1950).

The New Spaniards, John Hooper. Penguin, 1994.

The Fabled Shore, Rose Macaulay. Oxford University Press, 1986.

The Spanish Temper, V.S Pritchett, V S. Hogarth, 1984.*In Spain*, T. Walker. Corgi, 1989.

Right: fiesta flags provide decoration and shade

Practical Information

83

GETTING THERE

By Air

By Sea

TRAVEL ESSENTIALS

When to Visit

By Rail

By Road

Visas and Passports

INSIGHT
Pocket Guides

Insight Pocket Guides pioneered a new approach to guidebooks, introducing the concept of the authors as "local hosts" who would provide readers with personal recommendations, just as they would give honest advice to a friend who came to stay. They also included a full-size pull-out map. Now, to cope with the needs of the 21st century, new editions in this growing series are being given a new look to make them more practical to use, and restaurant and hotel listings have been greatly expanded.

ACKNOWLEDGEMENTS

Photography	**Robert Mort** *and*
22B, 32, 38B, 82	**J.D. Dallet**
6B, 6T, 7B, 12, 29, 21, 28, 35, 50, 55,	
62, 63, 64B, 70, 85, 90	**Nick Inman**
54	**James Davis Travel Photography**
10	**Instituto Geografico Nacional**
13	**Oronoz**
7T, 16, 25, 26B, 26T, 30, 34, 36T,	
41T, 57, 61, 75, 81, 83, 87	**Prisma**
14	**Jan Read**
5	**Mark Read / APA**
1, 2–3, 41B	**Robert Harding Picture Library**
86	**Topham Picturepoint**
94	**Trip / E & J Bradbury**
36B, 92	**Gregory Wrona**
Front cover	**Pictures Colour Library**
Back cover top	**Oronoz**
Back cover bottom	**J.D. Dalet**

Cartography	**Maria Donnelly**

The author would like to thank the Agència Valenciana del Turisme and the Consejería de Turismo y Cultura de Murcia for their help with the updating of this book.

INDEX

Accommodation 93–5
Agost 38–40, 44, 45, 72
Agres 28
Alcalà de la Jovada 28
Alcantarilla 60
Alcoi (Alcoy) 12, 14, 23, 24–5
Aledo 65
Algueña 45
Alhama de Murcia 61, 65, 75
Alicante (Alacant) city 14, 27, 35–8
    Barrio Santa Cruz 37
    Calle Mayor 37
    Calle San Isidro 36
    Casa Consistorial 36
    Castillo de Santa Bàrbara 35, 48
    Dársena restaurant 38, 75
    eating out 75
    Museo Alicantino de Arte Contemporeneo
    (MACA) 37
    Museo Arqueologico de Alicante 35–4
    Museo de Belenes 37
    Museo de Bellas Artes Granne
        (MUBAG) 37
    nightlife 38, 78
    Nit del Foc fiesta 36
    Nou Manolín restaurant 36, 75
    Peret's kiosk 38
    Playa del Postiguet 36
    Pozos de Garrigós 37
    San Nicolás cathedral 36
    Santa María church 37
    shopping 71, 72
    Tossal de Manises (Lucentum) 35
Almansa castle 49
Alquerías 60
Altea la Vieja (La Vella) 30
Archena 59, 61
art and crafts 38–40, 72
    Centro Regional de Artesanía (Lorca)
        64–5
    potteries 39–40
Azorín 45

Bañeres (Bañyeres de la Mariola) 49
Baños de Mula 61
Barranc del' Encanta 28
beaches 83

Beniardá 30
Benidorm 32–3
    eating out 75
    nightlife 32, 33, 78–9
Beniel 60
Benimantell 29
Benissa 21
Biar 49
Blanca 59
Bocairent 28
Borgia (Borja) family 30–31
Bullas 58, 66
bullfighting 80
business hours 93

Cabo de la Nao (Cap de la Nau) 22
Cabo de las Huertas 37
Cabo de Palos 68, 69, 75
Cabo de San Antonio (Cap de San Antoni)
    22
Calasparra 58–9
Calblanque 68, 69
Callosa d'Ensarriá 23
Calpe (Calp) 21, 27, 71
camping and caravanning 95
Caravaca de la Cruz 66
car hire 91, 92
Cartagena 11–12, 14, 67–8
    Byzantine Wall 68
    Castillo de la Concepción 67
    Catedral Atigua 68
    Columbus restaurant 68
    La Tartana restaurant 68, 76
    Museo Arqueológico Municipal 68
    Museo Nacional de Arqueología Marítíma
        68
    Nuestra Señora de los Remedios 68
    Roman theatre 68
Castalla 76
Cehegin 66
children 89
Chinchilla castle 49
Cieza 59
Cocentaina 12, 13, 23–4
    eating out 76
Col de Rates 23
communications and media 97–8